THE INCREDIBLE
SHERLOCK HOLMES
PUZZLE
COLLECTION

THE INCREDIBLE
SHERLOCK HOLMES
PUZZLE
COLLECTION

JOEL JESSUP

This edition published in 2024 by Arcturus Publishing Limited
26/27 Bickels Yard, 151–153 Bermondsey Street,
London SE1 3HA

AD011509NT

Printed in the UK

CONTENTS

INTRODUCTION

Many of my adventures with Sherlock Holmes have involved being in strange places at strange times, so when I tell you this one began with us both standing on the roof of a public house in Wapping at 2am, investigating the death of an old cat, you must understand that it was not even in the slightest the most odd activity we had ever done.

Holmes had summoned me from my bed to break into a warehouse and then climb from its uppermost window onto the roof of The Prospect of Whitby because Charlie, a legendary local cat beloved by the dock workers, had been murdered there. A curious Holmes had examined the feline corpse and had concluded it could only be the work of our mutual enemy, and former second-in-command of Moriarty, Colonel Sebastian Moran.

"The angle and nature of the cat's wound pointed to the conclusion that the blade that had killed it was thrown with remarkable skill," Holmes had explained as we moved through the warehouse.

"But Moran was a shot, not a knife-thrower!" I exclaimed, but Holmes pointed out Moran was in fact well versed with every form of assassination. He had escaped Newgate Prison only three months previously and Holmes now believed him to be hidden in the attic of the building we stood upon.

Holmes passed his hands over the surface of the roof before he found a concealed hatch. He pulled it back and we peered within. It was too dark to see inside until a sudden burst of moonlight enabled us to see the outline of a figure prostrate on a mattress.

I drew my Adams and prepared to cover any escape as Holmes braced himself to enter before suddenly stopping.

"Give me your gun, Watson," Holmes said casually, and I handed it to him. He aimed carefully and fired a single shot into the figure below! We heard a strange snapping sound.

"I think we can descend now," Holmes said.

As we entered, the floor was covered with horsehair. The body on the mattress was clearly a dummy, and in the middle a triggered foothold trap.

"Moran has already departed," Holmes said, "and he was conscious enough of our pursuit to leave us this nasty little surprise that was supposed to injure whoever tried to leap upon him."

We decided that our best recourse was to examine what was left behind. Moran could elude our capture but not Holmes' keen observation.

The next morning I visited Baker Street and found Holmes poring over the items from Moran's bolthole. As I entered, he smiled at me with a glint of excitement in his eye.

"Ah, Watson. Tell me what you make of this…"

From the table Holmes picked up a playing card and showed me. It was the four of Spades.

"A playing card? From Moran's hideaway. He is after all a professional card cheat. No doubt you have observed some unusual element of it that I have overlooked."

"I have indeed, but I don't fault you for not seeing it, because it isn't its appearance that made me realize its secret, but its texture…"

He took the card in a pair of tongs.

"A hidden image has been carefully printed on it with a compound, possibly cerium oxalate. Hence the thicker, rougher texture."

He carefully dipped the card into a beaker of clear liquid.

"You simply have to expose it to a solution of hydrogen peroxide and manganese sulfate…" He removed the card and showed me how its images had been replaced by a curious series of symbols. "…And a secret is revealed!"

"How did you know this solution would work?" I said.

"The truth is that Moran had this liquid in a hip flask. Once I realized the cards were unusual and the flask did not contain alcohol, it made logical sense that one would activate another…"

"Wait, cards plural?"

Holmes showed me a deck of cards spread out across the table. He had already treated them all and each had different symbols and images, some with accompanying text.

I began to understand the significance of this mystery.

"Holmes, Moran's clever behind a rifle or with his knees under a card table, but this is beyond him!"

"Yes, I think the deck was given to him by his former employer."

"You mean… Moriarty?"

Holmes peered at the symbols on the cards.

"Yes, I'm sure this is his deck."

"He survived the falls? Impossible!"

"You once said the same of me, and yet here I am! However it's also possible Moran received these before Moriarty's death."

"But what do they mean?" I said.

"I'm not sure yet," said Holmes, "Why would Moriarty create them? Perhaps they contain instructions to Moran, or possibly another agent of his, but in the past he has been very forthright about his control of his empire and didn't need such tricks."

"The empire you destroyed, you mean?" I said, and Holmes pantomimed modesty. "Holmes, if Moriarty is alive he would need to conduct his business in a clandestine manner to ensure he wouldn't be thwarted by you again. Perhaps he thinks codes and riddles are the only way he can achieve that."

"Yes, each card could be the key to a crime, or a criminal, or simply a target. But you must remember Moriarty's incredible intellect Watson. This may in fact be a trap designed to preoccupy me. There's only one way to find out."

Holmes put the cards into Moran's monogrammed playing card case. "We *must* solve every card in Moriarty's diabolical deck!"

Note on solving the puzzle cards

Each puzzle within the deck of cards corresponds to the story within of the same number. You may attempt to solve the puzzle by simply looking at the card. Or you may read the story which contains hidden messages and hints at the end.

Some cards are marked with a Sigma symbol (Σ). These hold special significance and overall point to a location where Moriarty's plan will come to fruition and that Sherlock must find before it is too late. Can you reveal it too?

PUZZLES

Puzzle 1
FORGERY

Details of a supposed Thomas Bewick
illustration, all wrong!

Except for one. Which?

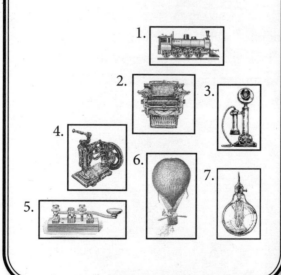

As I stared at the many cards, I couldn't see any grand connection between their contents. Holmes, as usual, spoke as if he had read my thoughts.

"Perhaps there is no connection, Watson. This may have been a sort of *aide-mémoire* for our mathematician friend, an encrypted inventory of information pertinent to his business. Plans for future crimes? Records of past crimes? I don't know yet."

He gathered them all together into a tidy deck and placed them next to the pristine typewriter he had received as a gift for his role in the resolution of the Marweather poisoning, still in its dustcover.

"What I do know is that Moriarty considered me to be an impediment. So I cannot discount the possibility that this is designed to distract me from some other scheme. An agitating little voice in my ear, like a telephone. For that reason I won't dedicate myself to their solution, simply carry them with me and when in the normal course of our activities I think of an answer for one I will complete it on the spot, as it were."

"Well, I look forward to being on a thundering train with you, attempting to subdue the Great Eastern Strangler, and then having you suddenly unhand him and pull out a playing card shouting, 'The answer is 43, of course!' as he grabs me round the throat…"

Holmes gave me an affectionate smile, "I will, of course, be prioritizing any situation where life and limb is at peril. I think you can rely on me to run on several tracks at once."

Fanning the deck out, he picked a single card from it and showed me. It seemed to be a printing of individual details from an illustration. A note underneath said the images proved the supposed Thomas Bewick picture was a forgery, except for one.

"Here's one I have already solved, despite the damnable distraction of Mrs. Hudson's sewing machine clattering away downstairs. What do you think, Watson?"

"Well, I don't know if Bewick was in the business of putting his pictures on playing cards…"

"Come on my dear old friend, need I spell it out in Morse Code? Thomas Bewick first came to fame in 1797 with *History and Description of Land Birds*. I have a copy here somewhere; it's well rendered, if out of date. He died in 1828, before many of the supposedly miraculous devices with which we have filled our world were invented..."

I further examined the card.

"Is the art not up to Bewick's usual standards?" I ventured.

"Not at all! As you know, I've written several monographs on the subject of wood-engraving forgeries. These images are the finest work I've ever seen."

"So it must be something about the images themselves," I surmised, examining the details of the card and waiting for a light to go on in my head. "One image, Watson. A particular device that does something that nothing else can do... Yet."

Hints
Thomas Bewick was an illustrator in the late 18th century.
All but one of the things in the pictures were invented in the 19th century.

Puzzle 2
RAILWAY TIME

It is 1891. These station times are correct. What time is it at London Charing Cross Station?

Gare Du Nord
Paris, France

Middleton Station
Wellington, New Zealand

Potsdammer Banhof
Berlin, Germany

Charing Cross Station
London, England

Holmes had kindly invited me along to have dinner with a friend and distant relative of his, Monsieur Lhermitte, a French gentleman who was in London to investigate the possibility of opening an establishment here. We dined together at Kettners' in Soho, which always offered an excellent meal and lovely atmosphere.

But Holmes hungered not for food but the company of his friend.

"15 minutes late?" said Holmes. "This is unusual."

"Is he never late?" I asked.

"No, he is usually precisely five minutes early. My friend is a connoisseur not only of food but of speed… In fact he is accustomed to cooking while moving at great speed. One might call it fast food."

I imagined a chef cooking an omelette on horseback.

A thought struck Holmes and he produced the familiar deck of cards.

"Another solution, Holmes?" I asked.

"Another solution, Watson. This particular puzzle makes use of the disparity of time measurement between here and other countries. Our Greenwich Mean Time has stamped a wax seal on the scroll of chronology, and though our friends abroad may dislike it, they have no choice but to adopt a recognizably fixed point."

"Even if they recognize GMT to be entirely accurate, they are the ones who decide how much to add or subtract," I commented.

Holmes nodded. "That's true. But you'll note that Paris time is not 10 hours in advance of ours despite how much our governments dislike each other. Having your average peasant *fermier* toiling in the fields at 2am just to cock a snook at the Royal Observatory is beyond even Monsieur Sadi Carnot."

I leaned forward to read the card in question but it was at this point that M. Lhermitte arrived.

"Gentlemen, je suis vraiment désolé!" he uttered, sliding into the chair. "Truly sorry for my lateness. I regret it is my own fault. If I had not paid the driver extra money to spur his carriage on to a

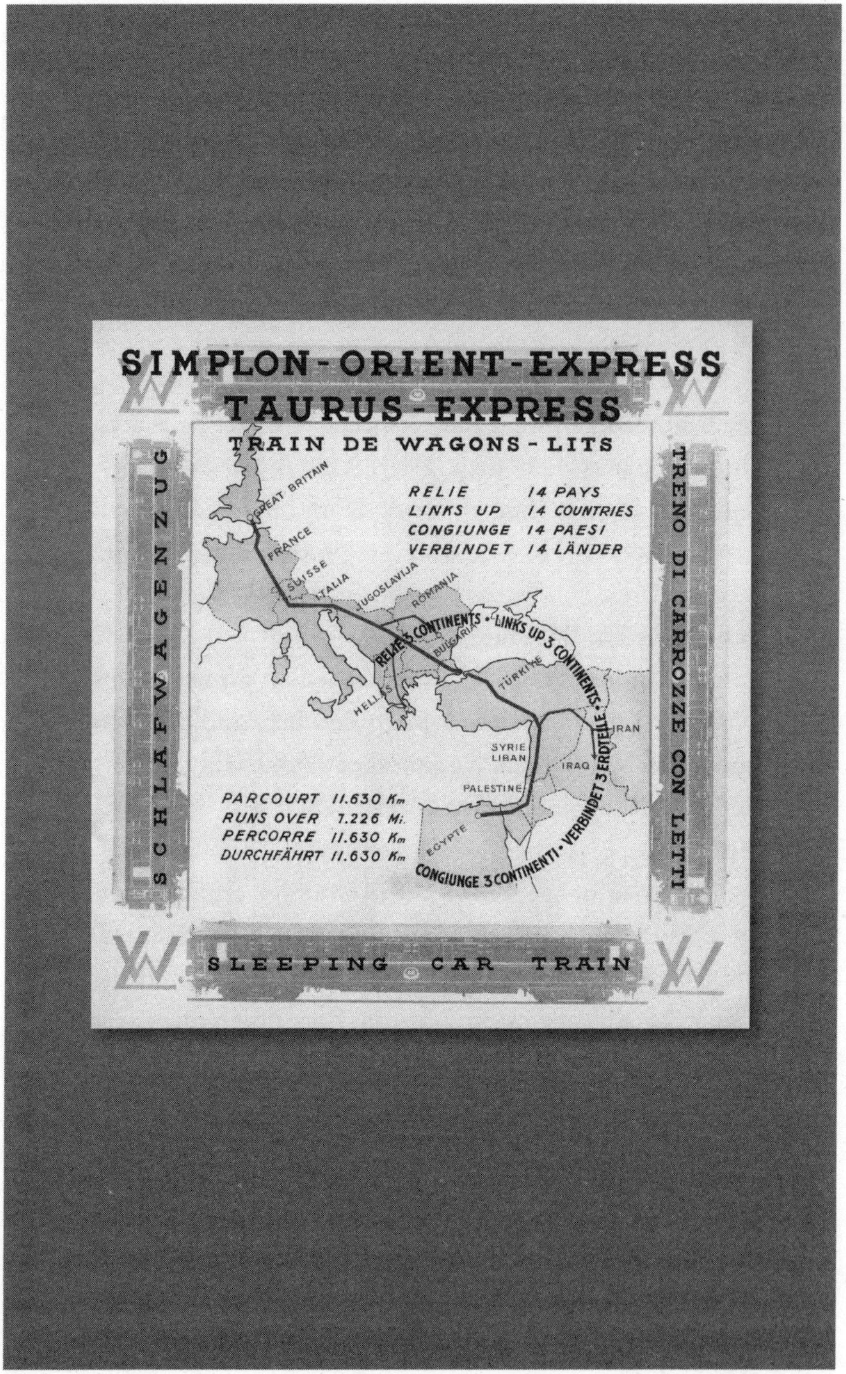
SIMPLON-ORIENT-EXPRESS
TAURUS-EXPRESS
TRAIN DE WAGONS-LITS
RELIE 14 PAYS
LINKS UP 14 COUNTRIES
CONGIUNGE 14 PAESI
VERBINDET 14 LÄNDER
GREAT BRITAIN
FRANCE
SUISSE
ITALIA
JUGOSLAVIJA
ROMANIA
BULGARIA
HELLAS
TÜRKIYE
IRAN
SYRIE LIBAN
IRAQ
PALESTINE
EGYPTE
RELIE 3 CONTINENTS • LINKS UP 3 CONTINENTS • VERBINDET 3 ERDTEILE • CONGIUNGE 3 CONTINENTI
PARCOURT 11.630 Km
RUNS OVER 7.226 Mi.
PERCORRE 11.630 Km
DURCHFÄHRT 11.630 Km
SCHLAFWAGENZUG
TRENO DI CARROZZE CON LETTI
SLEEPING CAR TRAIN

great speed, we would not have thrown a wheel at Pall Mall the way we did."

"You shouldn't have worried about being late," I proffered.

"At that point I was not late," he said, hanging his head, "I simply wished to see how fast the vehicle could go." Holmes rubbed Lhermitte's shoulder in a reassuring fashion.

I remembered Holmes' comment about Lhermitte's cooking at high speed and asked the question. The Frenchman sat up proudly.

"I am the chief caterer on the Orient Express! No-one else can produce such delicious cuisine at 125km an hour!"

Now I understood why Holmes' friend was always five minutes early. Clocks inside Paris train stations were deliberately set five minutes behind the clocks on the outside, so that the French might not miss their trains.

"Congratulations! And now you wish to start a restaurant here?"

"Oui, that is mon plaisir. I wish to cook without moving at high speed. My heart is not what it was, and then it will be murder on the Orient Express, mon brave."

Hints
The feelings of the French toward time (GMT).
France deliberately sets clocks five minutes early to avoid people missing trains.

Puzzle 3
DYNAMICS OF AN ASTEROID

Match the letters and numbers

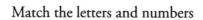

1.

2.

3.

A. B. C.

Σ

In his other life as a "humble" mathematician, Moriarty's biggest contribution was his book, *The Dynamics of an Asteroid*, theoretically so mathematically "pure" that no man was capable of criticizing it because they could never understand it. Many mathematicians claimed they *did* understand it, but had probably not even unwrapped their copy.

Holmes himself had attempted it several times, but he was not a master mathematician and as such found it as impenetrable as your average street vendor might.

"My opinion of it is that it is either a genuinely sound collection of mathematical reasoning, or it is something akin to an elaborate prank on Moriarty's part," said Holmes as he leafed through. I noted he had one of the cards from the deck next to him and was comparing it to a chapter apparently about celestial objects blocking the view of others.

"Then why try to read it?" I suggested. "If it's false then it's simply a waste of time, and if it's accurate then I suggest it is of limited use to you, unless we find ourselves on an asteroid one day."

"Two reasons. One is that I now wonder if there might be some kind of codes hidden within the text."

"You mean even his mathematical work served his criminal objectives?"

"Perhaps. The other is that this card reminded me of some aspects of it. Particularly those regarding the importance of location in perception. Where you are affects what you see."

"And are there any codes?"

Holmes flung the book to the table.

"In all honesty, I haven't the foggiest!"

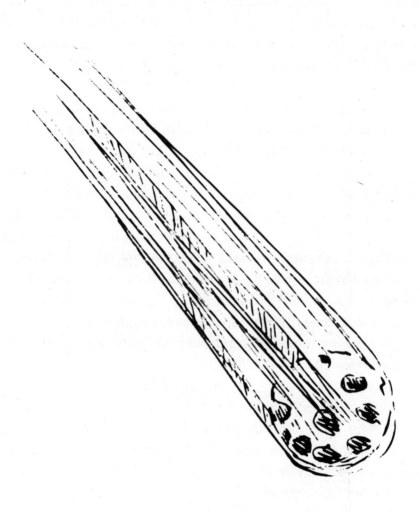

Hints
Some objects block or obscure others.
Try to imagine what you might see from that angle.

Dynamics of an Asteroid

Puzzle 4
PIANOFORTE

Which keyboard is correct?

A.

B.

C.

"Elizabeth Carlton-Rose?" Holmes asked the practically dressed young woman in front of us.

"Dr. Carlton-Rose, if you please," she said without looking up from dismantling what seemed to be a piano's keyboard, with its long white keys and short black keys, somehow connected to mechanical parts.

"What is your field of study?" Holmes asked.

"Pneumatics, Mr. Holmes. At the University of London, the other students would call me a windbag, if they bothered to address me at all…"

Holmes had accepted a commission from Professor Archibald Meath, who had lost two valuable geodes. The case intrigued him because the professor had been travelling with them in his briefcase at the time, and it would take a very deft fingersmith to successfully pull two huge crystalline rocks from a locked bag. The professor had only noticed when he found his flask of tea had leaked and had damaged some papers.

He had immediately accused Dr. Elizabeth Carlton-Rose, who worked in the office next to him at the Natural History Museum. He had complained to her of loud noises and grease stains in the corridor.

"I'm surprised Meath can hear anything through the big bushes of ear hair he has cultivated," she scoffed.

"And the grease stains?" Holmes asked.

"I did not shadow him onto the train and magically transport two stones out of his bag! It seems more likely they were never in there at all."

Holmes considered this, then asked about the machine.

"It's what they call a 'player piano'. I'm seeing if pneumatic pressure could be used to read the music roll. My office at the South Kensington museum has rats, but they're less disruptive than here, with Meath banging the wall on one side and a massive temperature drop on the other for some reason."

We walked to that side of the room and agreed it was about 10 degrees colder.

Holmes nodded and we withdrew to the corridor to discuss. I voiced the opinion that, while she was quite impertinent, she was unlikely to have been able to commit the crime.

"Watson, after our adventure with… the woman… I have learned not to discount the abilities of any member of the opposite sex, even one eviscerating a piano."

"Wait, didn't Irene Adler also use a piano? She was called the 'Enchantress of the 88 keys'."

"Singers often do, Watson. No, I'm more interested in the office on the other side of Dr. Carlton-Rose…"

Ten minutes later a refrigeration expert named Herman Kaffler sheepishly handed the two missing geodes back to a grimacing Professor Meath. He had swapped them for two large chunks of ice as the professor left, as revenge for Meath's complaints about his appearance, accent and the smell of his lunches. It was not spilled tea in the bag but the ice-lumps melted to water.

I noted that neither man apologized to Dr. Carlton-Rose, but she seemed used to this treatment. Holmes later remarked, he knew who the true windbags were…

Hints
Shorter keys usually black, and vice versa.
Pianos have 88 keys.

Puzzle 5

WEIGHTS AND MEASURES

Balance the third set of scales perfectly,
using all the weights.

Gold   Silver   Iron

Holmes sat in his chair ferociously devouring a new book from the stage magician John Maskelyne, called *Sharps and Flats*.

"This book is the most comprehensive analysis of crooked gambling techniques I have read so far…" he enthused, "it is worth its weight in gold, which is the heaviest element, of course, save for Osmium."

"Is that the fellow who built the card-playing automaton?" I asked.

"Psycho? Indeed, although I am sure it is a hoax. Every time I have tried to see it performed, it seems they receive advance notice of my attendance and cancel it. I am worse than the rain at Lord's."

"Don't you tire of reading only about crime?" I asked, knowing the true answer.

"Why Watson, only last week I read three books about crop rotation!" he exclaimed.

"Only because you were tracking a ring of smuggling farmers," I countered.

I noted he was using one of the deck's cards as a bookmark. "You're getting a bit cavalier with those cards, aren't you?"

"There is no more appropriate place for this card than to mark a place in a book about marked cards and criminal enterprises," Holmes drily observed. "In fact this particular one touches on another, older form of magical chicanery… transmutation."

He showed me the card, with a series of weights and scales with different alchemical symbols. "Once you realize the three silver weights are worth four more than two iron weights, the answer is…"

"Elementary?" I ventured.

"…Alchemy, my dear Watson."

Hints

Golden Sun weighs one more than two Silver Moons.
Three Silver Moons are four more than two Iron Mars.

Puzzle 6

THE PATH OF LIGHT

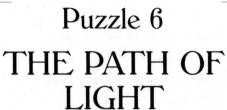

Match each beam to the appropriate optical device.

A. Convex lens   B. Concave lens
C. Mirror

1.

2.

3.

Σ

Holmes slumbered quietly in a chair beside me.

He'd meant to stay up all night as we watched the house of Ernest Trinder here in St. Helens. We suspected Trinder had kidnapped a boy from outside his school yesterday.

The boy's family were poor and no note was received, so ransom was not suspected. But when they found the body of a servant girl named Agnes Jones in the Sankey canal, Holmes saw a connection and had made his way here immediately.

He had examined pieces of waterlogged paper they had found on the body and scoured the scene of the boy's abduction. Another child had seen a distinctive squinting man near the gates and so we had decamped to this house, with local policemen hidden nearby. By this point Holmes had been awake for 34 hours so it was natural he would fall asleep.

When the rising sun hit Holmes' pair of Zeiss binoculars they focused a beam of light that struck him directly in the face! He woke instantly, reaching for the deck and finding a card.

"Watson, I have literally seen the light."

He waved the binoculars at me. "Lenses! Not only have I solved another card, but I realize that Mr. Trinder only travels during the day."

And indeed Ernest Trinder appeared on the street, carrying a big sack. Seeking to notify our hidden comrades, Holmes grabbed a shard of broken mirror and reflected the sunlight toward their hiding spot, from where they quickly leapt and grabbed Trinder. They pulled the sack open to reveal an unconscious, but living boy.

"You see Watson," Holmes began. "All the events, even poor Agnes' death, are connected."

"Why was Agnes Jones connected?" I asked.

"I suspected the waterlogged pieces of paper we found on her body were parts of a ransom note. But why would she have the ransom note for a child entirely unrelated to her or her employer?"

"She stole it?" I suggested.

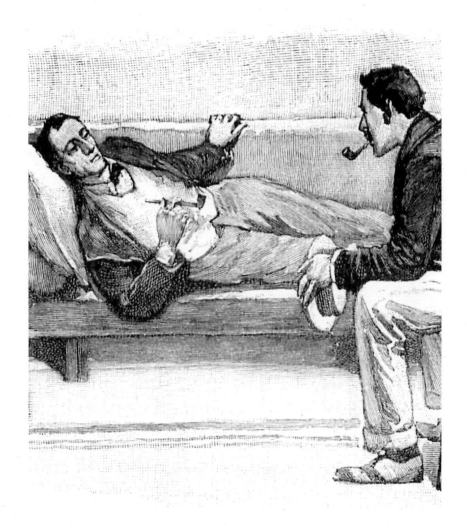

"I believe the note was delivered to the house where she worked at a time when her employer was in London. Trinder had in fact kidnapped the wrong child."

"Havisham has a son the same age? Who goes to the same school?"

"Precisely. Mr. Trinder sought to cover his gambling debts by taking a rich man's child, but accidentally kidnapped this poor boy. Then the unaware Trinder drops the ransom note at the Havisham household and I believe Miss Jones recognized his handwriting and sought him out demanding a cut of the ransom. Then perhaps she told him of his mistake and he decided to kill the messenger."

"But why does he travel only during the day?"

Holmes stared at Trinder, whose sour, twisted face had a distinct squint.

"Mr. Trinder has poor eyesight. He abducted the wrong child, did not realize Havisham was away, and most likely struggles to see at night. Unfortunate that he works at a glass factory… and yet is unable to afford spectacles."

Hints
The way the light travels through Holmes' Zeiss binoculars.
Holmes uses a hand mirror to signal to the local policemen to descend on the house.

Puzzle 7

ANUBIS' MAGIC SQUARE

What are the two missing hieroglyphs?

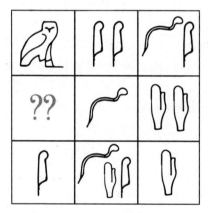

Holmes had been called to investigate a strange incident at the British Museum.

"At 9am Dr. Pierce Higgins felt a sharp blow to the back of his head. When he recovered, he found a burlap bag on the ground with an ancient crown inside," said Holmes as we walked swiftly through the galleries.

"He thought an intruder had coshed him and a nearby broken window seemed to confirm this."

"Why would the intruder leave the crown?"

"Or the entire case of valuable jewels nearby? Exactly. Additionally, the window is…"

Then Holmes suddenly stopped. We were standing in the sculpture gallery, next to the Rosetta Stone, the remarkable tablet written in three languages that enabled scholars to decipher the meaning of Egyptian hieroglyphics.

"Of course!" Holmes exclaimed, pulling out Moriarty's deck and extracting a card. It had a series of simplified hieroglyphs in a grid pattern, with many an empty space.

"I assumed that the symbols correspond to letters. But I see now that they must stand in for numbers!"

"You mean it's just a code, not real hieroglyphics?"

"Yes, I assumed he was being cleverer than I thought."

"Um, Holmes, are we expected?"

"Yes, of course," Holmes demurred and resumed his journey forward. "The window, I meant to say, was inaccessible from the ground due to its position and orientation, unless the burglar had wings and could squeeze through a three-inch gap."

He held up the card again. "Each of the squares has a different number value based on the symbols or combination therein! All the numbers are different so the empty square's number must also be unique! This owl represents one, the serpent is two…"

By then we had arrived in the storage room, where a soreheaded

Dr. Higgins stood. Holmes listened patiently to the doctor's reiteration of the story as he examined the crown.

"...and then I believe the authorities contacted you."

"Indeed they did. But you need not worry, Dr. Higgins. The bump on your head was not the product of an intruder. Look!"

Holmes turned the crown to show an oily stain on the crown's corner.

"See this?"

Higgins goggled.

"Is it blood?"

"No, dear fellow. Macassar oil. Your brand, I think. As unbelievable as it might seem, I suspect the extremely strong North-Easterly winds last night blew that window open, knocking this remarkably heavy

piece of ornamentation off its high shelf, where it bounced off your head, if you forgive the terminology, and landed in this sack, left by a careless workman. See the builder's mark on the edge, and the traces of clay inside the sack? No burglar. Simply bad weather."

Or an ancient curse, I thought. But I kept that to myself...

Hints
The symbols relate to numbers, not letters.
The owl represents one, the serpent is two.

Puzzle 8
KITE STRING

Kites with razor string not effective
for assassination.
Which is the correct end of the string?

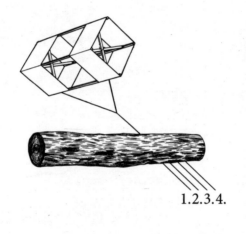

1.2.3.4.

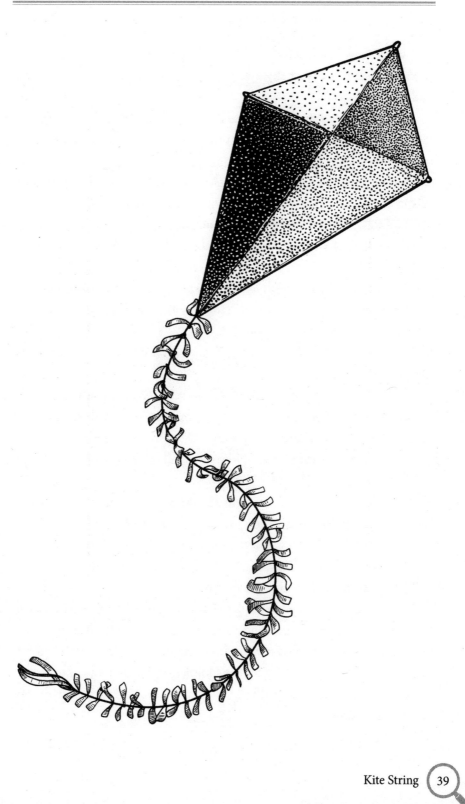

It was a sharp, cold wind that blew at the top of Parliament Hill. It was 5am and the clear sky offered a distant view of London. Holmes had brought a kite.

"I'm sure there's some clever reason for you to have that, Holmes," I commented, "but that doesn't diminish the strangeness of it, or of the image of you running along with one."

"Add yourself to that image, Watson, for it shall take us both to get this in the air."

"Holmes, I have faced down terrible dangers with you, but if I am seen here playing with kites, it will probably have a negative impact on my practice."

"Not at all Watson, your patients will no doubt be impressed by your vitality at an advanced age. Moriarty is older than you and he is interested in kites…"

He showed me a card from the deck with a kite and several pieces of string.

"It's not the one you think it is," he said. Rather presumptuous, I thought, but then I admitted to him that he *has* been able to practically read my mind in the past.

"Yes, I have," said Holmes. "Now you shall be the runner and I shall hold the string."

After satisfying myself there wasn't a crowd of onlookers, I took the kite and Holmes began running down the hill at a brisk, scientifically calculated pace, which I aspired to match.

"Did you make this kite yourself, Holmes?" I shouted over the wind.

"I did. I do not think they sell kites made of human skin at Hamleys!"

I know Holmes too well to think this anything other than a joke, luckily. It did not take long for the wind to catch the kite and lift it into the air quickly. Holmes controlled it with the string quite well and we stood for a moment watching it as I waited for Holmes to explain its significance.

He did not and eventually I snapped at him, "Holmes will you please explain this!"

"Very well Watson, it's perfectly simple: I am currently under observation by an agent of a foreign government. I presume I have accidentally stepped onto a tiny corner of their web while investigating another case but their tradecraft is excellent and I genuinely don't know to which country they pledge allegiance."

"And flying a kite will… solve that?"

"I know a… government consultant who can send someone to clear things up. But first he needs to know to which embassy he must send them. So I'm flying a kite and then, when one particular country's network is abuzz with news about it, my connection will know in whose ear to whisper."

"So really you could be doing anything strange? That *wouldn't* involve being up on a cold windy hill early in the morning?"

"Would you quarrel with a fletcher over how he makes his arrows? No, this action draws a clear line between the kite and our culprits… which is what the card requires as well."

Holmes took me to visit his brother Mycroft at his usual lair, the Diogenes Club, created in Pall Mall as a gentlemen's club for the anti-social and misanthropic. For that reason, speaking inside the building was forbidden except for in the Stranger's Room, which is where we had met him before, when he tasked Holmes with the case of the Greek Interpreter. Holmes had not told me of the reason for our meeting this time.

He was already in the chamber when we arrived, as broad as ever and, naturally, seated and looking fairly immovable. He smiled as we entered.

"Ah, Sherlock," he said, "have you been flying your kite again today? Obviously not, the wind speed is much diminished."

"You should try it, Mycroft. But you have my thanks for eliciting the help of your connection."

At this time I was unaware that Mycroft himself WAS the

connection, a node through which much of Whitehall's more mysterious needs passed. I merely thought him Holmes' idle older brother and government auditor.

"Yes, we must all admire the simplicity of the Japanese flag. But is that the only reason you wished to meet?" Mycroft asked, grunting slightly as he shifted position. "Or did you wish to consult me on the puzzles in Moriarty's deck of cards?"

Holmes sighed, as he often did when the barrels of his brother's equally enormous deductive skill were trained on him. "I have not mentioned anything of the sort to you, but I'm sure you would love to explain to Watson how you know of them."

"With pleasure. The cut of your jacket shows a lump the size of a pack of cards. You are not given to cardistry but I detect a slight staining on your fingers that suggests you have been handling these cards often. I remembered you have relented in your search for Sebastian Moran in the past couple of months so I postulated the cards were in his possession and they contain some clue to a bigger mystery that points to the late Professor."

He sipped his brandy and continued, "Also you've been seen peering at them in public. Often."

"I don't require your assistance with solving the cards, thank you, Mycroft. But I did want to show you this one."

He rifled through the deck, pausing briefly on one that had a series of flags with elements removed from them, to which Mycroft briefly, remarked "The sun always shines in Buenos Aires", and then found a different one, which I only briefly saw had a grid and a series of small thick lines, that he showed to Mycroft but not me.

"I'm sure you understand the significance of this?" he said.

Mycroft's mouth pressed into a thin line, "I do indeed. Thank you, Sherlock. I shall have to talk to someone at the Navy."

As we left, I briefly thought to ask Holmes about the card but he changed the subject swiftly.

Hints
It's not the one you might think.
Trace a line between them.

Puzzle 9

ATMOSPHERIC PHENOMENA

Which is which?

A. Waterspout

B. Aurora Borealis

C. St. Elmo's Fire

1.

2.

3.

Σ

Somehow, while journeying to the small village of Scrabster, our tent had been stolen, and therefore Holmes and I had to bunk down in the exposed air. Holmes did merrily point out that we needed to be out in the open anyway.

We had been summoned to the village by a concerning puzzle. Years earlier a resident had taken to poisoning people with mushrooms, giving them strange hallucinations before an agonizing death. The insane culprit had killed themselves upon discovery.

However, some concerned residents had recently complained of seeing strange lights in the sky, and they feared there was another poisoner! In hindsight, I should have seen the solution myself, especially considering the location of the lights and the location of the village.

The atmosphere there had become that of a witch hunt, and Holmes and I had made the journey to Scotland forthwith to resolve the issue immediately. He said he had an inkling of what was happening, saying only that I would see for myself.

As we sat in the field, I was suddenly amazed to see the sky filled with flowing lights, just as the villagers described! Yet I had deliberately consumed no food or liquid locally.

"Have we been poisoned, Holmes?"

"Not at all, Watson. This is a scientific phenomenon known as Aurora Borealis. It often occurs in places close to the top of the world. I saw it myself during my travels in the colder regions. It is rare in Scotland but unmistakable. Almost as beautiful as a water spout, a pressure-based phenomenon I witnessed near Persia. We can reassure the locals that no poison is entering their body, short of any natural poisons that they may choose to consume recreationally…"

Hints
Aurora Borealis is a light-based phenomenon.
Waterspouts are created by barometric pressure.

Puzzle 10
THE ORRERY

Which of the planets
below is Planet X?

Σ

Moriarty first earned the title of Professor as the Chair of Mathematics at University College Nottingham, but was compelled to resign due to the "dark chatter" about him.

"I suspect Moriarty cultivated the chatter himself," Holmes said as we walked up to what was Moriarty's former office. "It allowed him to move to London, to be at the middle of his spiderweb. And he could blame any future sinister associations on this same chatter."

The university had been mortified when Moriarty's true nature was exposed and had sought to distance themselves from him. The location of his former office was suppressed and it was turned into a storage area to discourage any grim tourism. When Holmes requested to examine the room, as part of his gathering of data on Moriarty's possible survival, they reluctantly acquiesced, provided he promised to keep a low profile.

We passed a chalkboard with MVEMJSUN written on it.

"The planets, Watson," Holmes said. "We used a mnemonic, 'Merry Veritable Educators May Justify Some Urgency'. Of course, they've discovered Neptune since, so perhaps it should be 'Etcetera... May Justify Some Unusual Nonsense' or some other rot."

As we approached, we could hear someone inside making a considerable racket. Possibly a cleaner? Holmes pushed open the door carefully to reveal Dr. Carlton-Rose, the scientist we had encountered weeks earlier at the Natural History Museum. She paused in her rummaging, but seemed unflapped by our presence.

"Oh hello!" she said cheerily enough, wiping her oily hands on a nearby cloth. "Fancy seeing you here!"

"Fancy," said Holmes icily. "Are the college aware you're here?"

"I should hope so, they brought me in! There's an old pipe-based pneumatic message system behind the wall here that's been making ominous noises. They wanted me to see if I could fix it before all the undergraduates ran off home scared of ghosts..."

It seemed like too large of a coincidence to me and I could sense Holmes felt the same way, but he gamely went on with the ruse.

"Are you aware of the previous occupant of this room?" he asked, taking an interest in the contents of her toolbag.

"If I wasn't before then this would have tumbled it for me," she said, handing Holmes papers covered in complex mathematical formulae. "A raft of mathematical mumbo-jumbo all initialled JM."

She then showed us a metallic capsule. "It was inside here, and this was the source of the pipes' blockage."

While Holmes perused the documents Dr. Carlton-Rose showed me big gouges in the capsule's metal.

"Someone tried to fish this out of the system with a crowbar! You wouldn't happen to know where the pipe leads, would you?"

We all tracked its path through the building until we found a large hole in the wall in a room with an elaborate orrery. I peered into the hole but Holmes seemed more interested in the model.

"This has nine planets, Watson," he removed a card from his pocket.

"Some have speculated on the existence of a ninth planet at the edge of the solar system, Holmes," I remarked, having read about it in *The Times*. "Identified only with a letter. Moving unseen, undetected, only perceivable because of its influence on other things."

"Not unlike…" said Holmes, peering at Dr. Carlton-Rose, before finishing his thought. "…Moriarty."

Hints
MVEMJSUN- *Merry Veritable Educators May Justify Some Unusual Nonsense*
(Mercury, Venus, Earth, Mars, Jupiter, Saturn, Uranus, Neptune).
Speculation on the existence of a ninth planet.

ANAMORPHOSIS

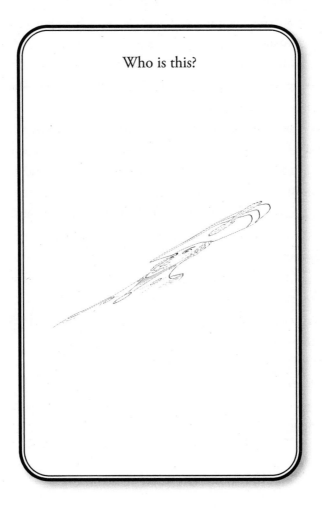

Who is this?

Holmes had invited me to join him at the National Gallery for the afternoon and we spent several hours observing and remarking on the excellent portraits.

We stopped in front of *The Ambassadors*, a two-man portrait painted by Hans Holbein the Younger in 1533. I was more familiar with Holbein from his role as a scout of sorts for Henry VIII, going around the world, painting beautiful girls from Spain to France and Germany, to find him a wife, but I admired the craftsmanship and strange esoteric details in this one, including an odd shape at the bottom of the painting.

"What is that?" I asked Holmes, but he had removed another card from the deck in his pocket and was nodding with recognition.

"The word, Watson, is anamorphosis. An image that seems unrecognizable until you look at it… from a certain point of view."

I tried squinting, moving back and forth and even, after a furtive check to see if we were alone, briefly turning my head upside down. Holmes was most amused by this.

"I suggest you move a little further down the gallery, Watson. This card doesn't require quite so much athleticism!"

I walked further and then, as I looked back at *The Ambassadors*, I saw the distorted image.

"A skull! But what is on the card?"

"A seafarer, Watson, a famous one. This very gallery is connected to a square that pays tribute to him! A coincidence? Perhaps not, considering also the location of Henry VIII's birth…"

Hints

It must be viewed at an angle.
It's a famous seafarer.

Puzzle 12
SHADOW GALLERY

What is wrong with the images?
How would you solve this?

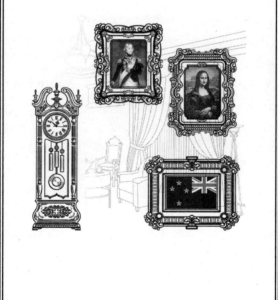

Holmes sat in apparent contemplation, staring at the surface of the river. We had just successfully exposed a smuggling gang in Limehouse and the main culprits had been taken away by the police.

"Reckon Lestrade would have given his left arm to have made this haul," said one constable jovially.

"With his conk, he looks enough like Nelson as it is!" replied another.

"Have some respect!" snapped Holmes, uncharacteristically. "And Nelson lost his right arm, not his left!"

He then wandered off and I learned he had gone down onto a pier and sat with his legs dangling over like a fisherman with no pole. He had not asked me to follow but he had also not forbade me to do so, so after 10 minutes I went and joined him.

"Ah, Watson," he said with apparent relief, "save me from my strange reverie. This river has not the charm of the Cam but it serves as a fair substitute."

Holmes was normally loath to discuss his youth but I knew that he had been educated at a college in Cambridge.

"I spent much of my time in my rooms, but very occasionally if the weather was fair I would travel alone to the river and sit on the banks."

"Staring at your own reflection?"

"Indeed. And one of the young men in the gang we just secured reminds me of myself. I am not taken to sentiment, but sometimes the paths, the riverways of one's life are exposed with an opposite image."

Hints

Lord Nelson lost his right arm, not his left.
You need to use a mirror.

Puzzle 13
THE MILLINERS

Which hats would be appropriate for a gentleman to wear in London?

1.

2.

3.

4.

5.

Holmes and I were in Lock & Co. on St. James' Street. I needed a new hat and Sherlock had decided to purchase it for me as he felt responsible. My most treasured hat had been run over by a cartwheel during the pursuit of an arsonist. My second choice was floating down the river Wye. And Holmes had used my last wearable hat to block the knife thrust of a surprisingly strong washerwoman who had been running a smuggling ring in Chelmsford.

"What about this, Watson?" Holmes queried, holding up a tweed deerstalker.

"I should look a bit foolish wearing a deerstalker around town, Holmes," I offered.

"I meant for the country, Watson, obviously," Holmes said. "I'm prepared to purchase you more than one hat."

"Thank you but I think deerstalkers in the country can be your preserve, Holmes. I don't think we should wear matching hats."

"What about this, sir?" said a little shopkeeper in a fez who seemed to have appeared like magic, and was holding out a mortar board towards me.

"I think wearing a mortar board around London would look even more foolish than a deerstalker," I suggested.

"My friend is not a teacher, despite his wise countenance," Holmes remarked.

In the end I selected a hard-wearing bowler in a striking maroon, and it was my preferred hat for all of three days before it was crushed underfoot by a rogue elephant at London Zoo.

Hints

You'd only find Holmes in a deerstalker in the countryside.
A mortar board would only be worn in academic circles.

Puzzle 14
DANCING MEN?

Decipher the code.

Holmes needed to meet with an unusual visitor to London and insisted that this particular person would only meet him at night, under a particular tree in Regent's Park.

"He is an American, and a secretive one," he explained as he picked the lock on the gates.

The man waited for us underneath a monolithic willow tree. Dressed fashionably and with a diminutive stature, he stood like a trained fighter and, as he lit a cigarette, his grey eyes were sharp and intelligent.

"Mr. Carter," said Holmes, shaking his hand.

"Call me Nick. Sorry about the cloak and dagger. I'd rather some people in London didn't know I'm not in New York. And vice versa. We could've met in public wearing disguises, but I wanted to meet you as myself, if you know what I mean…"

"This, of course, is my companion, Dr. John Watson…"

"A good man to have at your side."

Holmes got to the point. "Your enciphered message said you could give me an update on Moriarty's Chicago connections."

"I read your monograph on ciphers so I knew you could decode what I'd sent. Moriarty arrived in Chicago in 1890 and learned that being some pumpkin in the UK doesn't mean anything when you're on Jack Quartz's turf."

I was struggling to follow Mr. Carter's slang.

"What I mean, gentlemen, is that if Moriarty is the 'Napoleon of Crime', then Quartz is the Duke of Wellington, and he made it very clear that, as long as *you* were sniffing at Moriarty's tail, they weren't interested, and told him so in little dancing men."

Quartz held up a crumpled piece of cloth that had a series of, as Carter said, little dancing men in a row, like a child's drawing. The ink was dark brown and Holmes inspected it.

"Dried blood."

"Yeah, this was formerly part of the jacket of one of Moriarty's men.

And the blood was formerly part of his body, before one of Quartz's goons liberated it with a sharp knife."

Holmes reached into his pocket and took out the deck, extracting a card that, I saw now, had the same dancing men on it.

"Another cipher, Watson. And now I know what this card says as well. It features the words THE, IS and NOT, and is polite but unfriendly."

(Years later Holmes encountered the same cipher on a case, but he asked me to claim ignorance of it in my account, to preserve Mr. Carter's secrecy.)

Nick Carter eyed the deck with interest, "Did Moriarty make those?"

"I'll show you... if you explain why you're really in London," said Holmes significantly.

They locked eyes for a second, then Carter shook his head smiling.

"I'm sure you already know. I'll take a rain-check. Hope I was helpful. At least your nemesis is at the bottom of a waterfall."

"Good luck, Mr. Carter. And if I'm ever in New York, maybe we can meet... in daylight hours."

Hints
It's a substitution cipher.
It contains the words THE, IS and NOT.

Puzzle 15
CONSTELLATIONS

What are the constellations?

A. Leo   B. The Plough
C. Orion's Belt

Then calculate
Plough x Orion's Belt + Leo

1.

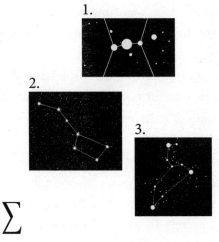

2.

3.

Σ

Holmes had been visited by a powerful government minister. The minister had received an anonymous message, informing him that if he did not visit a particular series of public houses, in a particular order, within a particular time frame, his personal secrets would be revealed.

The minister felt compelled to comply, despite suffering from a bad case of gout. But he had asked Holmes to discreetly tail him to ensure his safety. Holmes was no bodyguard but he was intrigued by the request. So we had, at great speed, followed the minister to The Cricketers, The Wheatsheaf, The Dog & Duck and The Slaughtered Lamb in quick succession. By the time we reached The Lion in Kensington, the minister was exhausted and Holmes intrigued.

"Very interesting," he said, pulling one of the cards from his pocket. "The sign of this place is the constellation Leo. Also the case with The Plough in Fenchurch Street, which we will visit next. It has the distinctive line and bowl shape, the reason why Americans call it: 'The Big Dipper'."

"But why are we on this ridiculous chase? Did you see any observers or spies in these places?"

"Not at all, which only confirms my suspicions. They could be very cleverly disguised, but I doubt our mysterious taskmaster would have gone to so much trouble, as he was not expecting the minister to be accompanied by me."

"So what is going on?" I asked, as we entered yet another carriage and instructed the driver to take us to The Plough.

"I suspect the minister's anonymous tormentor is trying to hide a rotten apple in a barrel. To an untrained eye, the distribution of these public houses is random but I observe a general momentum, a direction, until it reaches The Orion's Belt in Bermondsey, at which point the momentum leads away. The planning inadvertently reveals that this is where the trick, whatever it is, will be played."

And so it was. As soon as we entered The Orion's Belt, moments behind the nearly exhausted minister, Holmes immediately spotted the

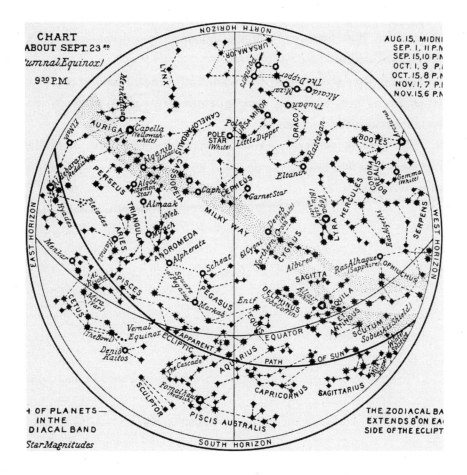

mechanism of the swindle. Several gentlemen bustled through the pub, 'drunkenly' bumping into the minister and swapping his fob watch for an ingenious replica.

I did not see the exchange, and was only aware of it because Holmes subsequently showed me the fob watch, having quickly pick-pocketed it himself from the original criminals! The confused and empty-handed gang were then apprehended by a brace of constables that Holmes had secretly requested.

"Thank you, Mr. Holmes," the minister wheezed as my friend returned the fob watch. "It is of great value to me…"

"And to the country, I should imagine, considering the secret documents within."

The minister was amazed but wasted no time in hailing a cab to return home and, no doubt, sleep an entire day. I asked Holmes how he knew about the documents.

"The watch's pattern contains several constellations, and the number of the stars hides a code. Now let us get a beer… somewhere more welcoming."

Hints

Orion's belt is a straight line, the plough has a big bowl shape like a dipper.
You need to use the number of stars in each constellation for the sum.

Puzzle 16
HMS *KNIGHT*

HMS *Knight* must eliminate these three "submarine ships" by moving onto all of their squares. It starts at A1 and can only move in the manner of a knight chess piece: either two horizontal then one vertical, or two vertical then one horizontal. What combination of moves would allow you to "sink" all three submarines?

	1	2	3	4	5	6	7	8	9	10
A								■		
B								■		
C										
D			■							
E			■							
F			■							
G							■	■	■	
H										
I										
J										

∑

Having not seen Holmes for a month, I was surprised when I received, in the mail, one of the cards from Moriarty's deck. The postmark said Bristol, but there were no other details beyond my address, not even an accompanying note.

It was the card that Holmes had shown his brother but had been reluctant to show me. It depicted three submarines, and a battleship, HMS *Knight*, that was required to eliminate them.

I could not see what was inherently dangerous about this card. The concept of submarines as a tool of war has existed for a long time, though never very usefully implemented. It might be that Holmes suspected Moriarty of having secret information regarding some submarine programme that the Navy was engaged in but I saw nothing on the card that indicated some special knowledge. And who sent this to me? I hoped it was Holmes though I couldn't think why. The alternative was someone else had got hold of this card, or even the entire deck, which might imply Holmes was somehow in danger. But why send it with no note?

With no answer to these questions, I set to work trying to solve the puzzle, finding it was prudent to write down which squares could "reach" the submarine squares using the knight's move. It was still fiendishly difficult.

Suddenly there was a sharp knock at the window of my study and I turned to see Holmes peering determinedly through. I motioned for him to go round to the entrance but he shook his head and I opened the window.

"I see you received it. Excellent."

"I am relieved to learn it was you who sent it, but why?"

He leaned in, "As a matter of fact, I was pursuing my thoughts about nautical connections at a shipyard in Bristol when I just happened to bump into our friend Dr. Elizabeth Carlton-Rose…"

"Surely not! She followed you?"

"She claimed she was aiding with some kind of pneumatic pump

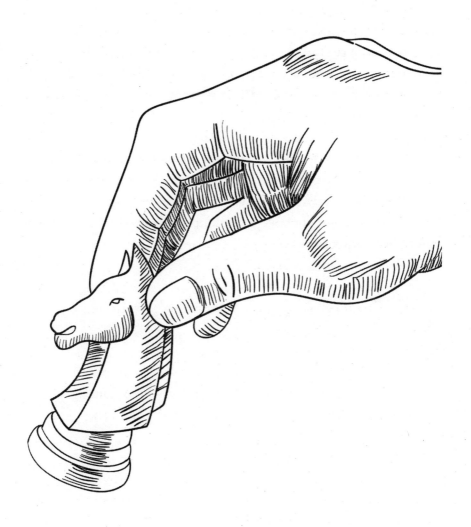

system but the coincidence is too large. She quickly showed me papers that indicated her presence was permitted, but it struck me she could have easily purloined them from someone else…"

"Then why and how did you mail me the card?"

"Considering the papers indicated skill at pickpocketing, and the crowded circumstances of our meeting, I was concerned she may take an opportunity to steal the deck, and – as I felt this particular card is too sensitive – I had to act fast. I went into a nearby clerk's office and put the card in an envelope with your address on it, concealing it in their mail bag."

"Did she get the cards?"

"No, I managed to take a shortcut. A1 to C2 to E3, as it were. In retrospect, perhaps my actions were rash. What if someone had intercepted the letter?"

"I think, the next time we bump into the lady, we should have a frank conversation with her."

"What a novel idea, Watson."

Hints
It helps to write down which squares can "reach" the submarine squares.
A1 to C2 to E3.

70 HMS *Knight*

Puzzle 17

A NEW SYMBOLOGY

Which symbol fills the last place in the grid?

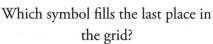

1. 2. 3. 4. 5. 6. 7. 8.

Edmund Bowley was a flamboyant-looking fellow, his huge blonde moustaches and bristling beard rounding his face almost like a lion's mane. Yet it was one of the most miserable faces I have ever seen. He had practically blustered into the flat, admitted by Mrs. Hudson just as Holmes was in the process of explaining how combining the first two symbols would create the third.

"I'm a proprietor of confectionary, Mr. Holmes. I have a shop in Cambridge and a good life… but I am hunted and haunted, Mr. Holmes. Pursued by figures the police are powerless to stop."

For the past week or so, everywhere he had gone, he had seen shifty-looking figures lurking just out of sight: when leaving his house, attending his shop, even going to church. Any attempt to confront the figures led them to immediately disappear. Bowley had reported this to the police but they had said that, in the absence of actual actions, there was nothing they could do.

"So I remain with a sword of Damocles hanging over my head, or should I say, scissors of Damocles!" he said tearfully.

"Why scissors?" said Holmes, his interest growing.

"Oh I don't know, sometimes they seem to be holding scissors or shears or something. I'm so tired. I cannot sleep for fear of them coming into my room!"

"Are you well known in your community?" asked Holmes, staring at Bowley's chin.

"I… should say so, I think. People seem to like me. We even used a poster of me to promote my shop, the employees suggested it."

Understanding crossed Holmes' eyes, "When was this poster erected?"

"… last week, now that you mention it…"

"And is your shop near or opposite a college?"

"Mr. Holmes, it's Cambridge, it is impossible not to be!"

Holmes leaned forward and put his hand on Bowley's shoulder.

"Then relax, sir. Your suffering is at an end. You must simply replace the poster with another one bearing this text."

Holmes quickly wrote something on a notepad and presented Bowley with it. As Bowley looked, his eyes widened and the gloomy little face blossomed into a sunny smile.

"Of course!" he beamed, and laughing to himself, practically danced out of the room. Holmes casually lit his pipe.

"So Watson… identical elements will be removed, and differing elements retained!"

"Holmes, you can't expect to simply return to the puzzle and not tell me what you wrote on that paper!"

"Come now Watson… His beard, his poster, scissors, college… what do you think?"

I thought, "Perhaps… the new poster should say that any students hoping to win the bet of getting a lock of Edmund Bowley's amazing beard will be prosecuted in the strongest possible manner?"

Holmes smiled, "Actually I suggested they would be banned from the shop. I feel that might be more effective…"

Hints

The third symbols are a result of the first two.

Identical elements are removed and differing elements are retained.

NO PUZZLE?

At his laboratory table in Baker Street, Holmes was deep in analysis of a particular type of clay that he said would help identify a manufacturer of counterfeit Wedgwood china, and he was allowing me to look through the deck of cards. As I did so, I suddenly came across one that looked like a simple playing card.

My first thought was that somehow a real card had accidentally been put into the pack. Then I remembered that, before they were treated, all of the cards looked like this.

"Did this card not react to the special treatment you created?" I asked Holmes, holding it up.

"It did not," Holmes admitted.

I saw he had written, "What's wrong with this?" on the card.

"Is this a note to yourself?"

"No, to you, dear Watson. For you see, the card did not need to change appearance, it is already a puzzle."

I peered at it further.

"Wait, this is both a King and a Queen…"

Holmes looked up from his studies, "I am not sure if Moriarty intended for me to continue trying different treatments on it, or expected me to immediately notice the defects, or some other outcome. Until I solve all the puzzles, I think his broader intentions will remain mysterious."

"Dealing with your mysterious intentions is often enough for me," I said, noting that there was something a little odd about the Queen's face.

"She actually looks a little like Sebastian Moran…" I said.

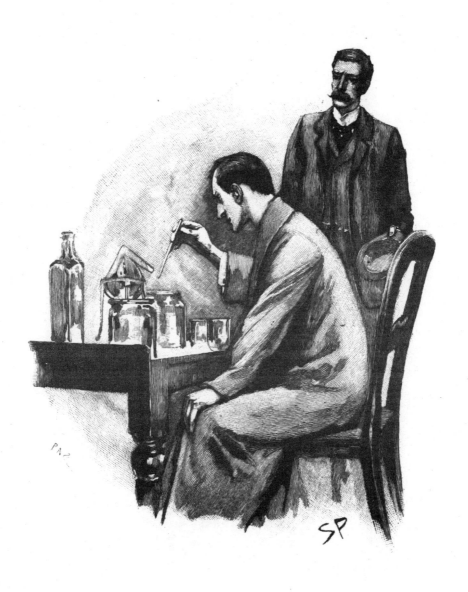

Hints

It's a King and a Queen together.
The suits are wrong.

Puzzle 19
SERPENTS

Which snake matches the
example below?

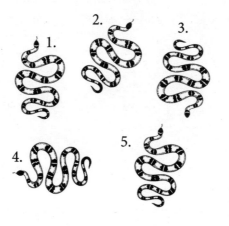

We had been asked by Inspector Lestrade to inspect a body that had washed up in St. Katharine Docks in Wapping, near Moran's former den in The Prospect of Whitby. But the victim had not been shot.

"Is this a snake bite, Mr. Holmes?" Lestrade asked, pointing to a puncture wound on the ankle of the corpse, a rather rotund older gentleman.

"This wound could have been made by any number of small weapons, Inspector. I must gather more data."

Holmes looked at the skin pallor, inside the mouth, at the eyes and even at the fingernails.

"You don't think he was bitten by a snake?" asked Lestrade.

"HE WAS!" shouted a dirty and wildly bearded man who shambled towards us, pointing a gnarled finger at the body.

"The fiend bit Reg, I seen it with me own two eyes!"

"You know this man?" Lestrade asked, regarding him with distaste.

"Yeah, 'e was always round here, sellin' this and that, all dodgy. No-one ever challenged him, he was bricky as the devil!"

"And a snake bit him?" I asked.

"'E showed it to me last night in a little cage, said 'e'd nicked it from some posh bloke. Then he drops it, cage breaks, he tries to grab it and it's on his ankle, quick as you like!"

"Do you know where it is?"

"In Hell, sir! I smashed it flat with me squeezebox. Can I get a replacement? You know, for bein' a hero?"

"What happened next?" asked Lestrade, ignoring the request.

"Well, he lurches back, doesn't he, shoutin', 'it's done for me!' And his face was all twisted up and he keels over off the dock!"

"And you didn't think to rescue him, or recruit others to do so?" I asked.

The bearded man looked sheepish, "Well I reckoned he was done for. I come and told you, didn't I?"

Serpents

"A poor excuse," said Lestrade. "This man could have lived if someone had drawn out the venom in time."

"There was no venom," said Holmes, standing up.

"So this toe-rag is lying?" asked Lestrade.

"Oh no, I fully believe 'Reg' was bitten. But it was most likely a dry bite."

Holmes explained how, if a snake thinks its victim is too big to consume whole, it won't waste venom on it and instead simply bite them. Lestrade and the others goggled.

"But he fell in the water!" said Lestrade.

"His corpse shows signs consistent with sudden stoppage of the heart. The only venom in his body was that of fear."

The bearded man was led away for questioning and I decided not to mention that he was wearing the striped snake as a belt. At least its tongue was not sticking out.

Hints
The number of stripes.
The tongue is not visible.

Puzzle 20
AGRICULTURE

Which one is actually
a vegetable?

1.

2.

3.

4.

5.

"Watson! Over 'ere!"

The cry penetrated across the crowded, noisy conurbation of Covent Garden Market, and I swiftly made my way towards its source, politely but firmly pushing my way past housekeepers, wholesalers sampling herbs, and competing teams of barrow boys.

I arrived at the packed stall, and behind it was a smiling man with a huge, if well-trimmed, beard, an enormous straw hat and a surprisingly big overcoat considering the warmer weather. As I approached, he gave me a familiar wink.

"Alright?"

I leaned closer to my disguised friend.

"Why are we here? I received your summons."

He looked around amongst the fruits and vegetables.

"Summons? Never 'eard of them. I got some tomatoes, lovely fruit."

Maybe Holmes was staying in character owing to the presence of some unseen onlooker.

"Tomatoes are a vegetable," I asserted.

"Oh no sir, a common misconfiguration. Same as with these beautiful pumpkins, actually fruit as well."

My elbow was jostled by a barrow boy.

"What's your name, sir?" the stallholder asked.

I paused, "You called me over? Watson?"

He chuckled, "No, sorry mate, I was calling Watson the barrow boy! 'Ere he is."

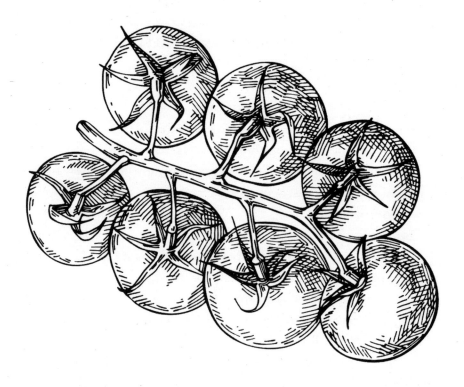

And I turned right to see what was clearly Holmes dressed as a barrow boy, giving me an amused look. I offered the stallholder my apologies.

"Mistook him for me, Watson?" he chuckled.

"Apparently you're now Watson as well," I countered.

"Yes, I borrowed your name. In the meantime, help me transport this rhubarb. A very interesting hardy perennial..."

Hints

Tomatoes are actually fruit, as are pumpkins.
Rhubarb may not be a fruit.

Puzzle 21
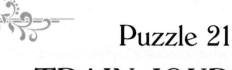

TRAIN JOURNEYS

Two trains leave for London simultaneously: one will travel 190 miles from Leeds, the other will travel 155 miles from Stoke-on-Trent.
The Leeds train makes two five-minute stops and the Stoke-on-Trent train makes four.
Both trains average 80mph.
Which arrives at King's Cross first?

Holmes had received word of an audacious plan: someone intended to steal The Flying Scotsman, the famed passenger service from King's Cross to Edinburgh!

"Is there something valuable on board?" I asked Holmes as we sat in a carriage barrelling along the road towards King's Cross.

"I'm not sure Watson. Something about this seems… odd," Holmes said, steepling his fingers.

"You think it's a lie? Or a feint to distract from something else?"

"No, the information came from a source that has impeccable judgement on these matters. A thief himself, although rather a principled one. And an excellent cricketer."

He had taken one of the cards out and was peering at it when he suddenly banged the roof of the carriage and then leaned out and shouted to the driver "STOP! We must go to Highgate Hill instead, immediately! Distance multiplied by speed!"

The driver, confused but sanguine, turned the vehicle around and headed in the alternative direction. Holmes smiled, "Often I find our encounters help me solve these cards but this may be the first time the card has helped me!"

He showed me the picture on it, of two trains, two cities and a puzzle of calculating speeds.

"The message said the train would be stolen. Not hijacked, not taken over, *stolen*. And they specified it would be stolen after *their* departure. You might call the people on a train 'their' but not the train itself."

As we approached Highgate Hill, Holmes gave the driver further instructions and we came to a stop in front of a small but well-appointed mansion house. Holmes leapt from the vehicle, leaving me to pay the driver, and had begun knocking ferociously on the front door when we suddenly heard what sounded like gunfire in the back garden! We could not enter as it was walled in with spikes and barbed wire, but then Holmes noticed the front door was now wide open! Entering cautiously, Holmes made his way towards a small set of stairs leading to the basement.

Hints

Distance times speed.
Remember to add the stops as delays.

As we entered, I saw a tiny model of a Scottish countryside, complete with trees, rivers, villages and people, and across it all tiny rail-tracks and tiny steam trains.

"This is H.K. Pennyweather's house and this is his famous model train set. Note all the little stops each train has to make."

Holmes spotted a large note pinned to the track, next to a facsimile of Edinburgh Station. He read the note.

"Dear Mr. Herlock Sholmes, congratulations on solving my crime! The Flying Scotsman is now a wedding present for my new bride, though it was the challenge of breaking into Mr. Pennyweather's supposedly impregnable house that was the real gift. You will have to hail a new carriage as I was driving your previous one. Thanks also for being distracted by the firecrackers I threw in the garden. Yours sincerely, M. Arsène Lupin, gentleman-thief."

Holmes screwed up the note and threw it at Edinburgh Station.

Puzzle 22

A HAND

What is the connection?

One of Holmes' greatest regrets was his inability to solve the murders supposedly conducted by "Jack the Ripper", although Holmes, of course loathed that jokey appellation.

"I cannot solve every single crime, even if that crime is both famous and terrible…" he would lament, "there simply isn't enough clear data."

This did not prevent members of the public attempting to either lambast him for not solving the murders, or, even more bafflingly, accuse him of collusion in them somehow, usually in the service of either the government or Queen Victoria. One of Moriarty's cards even seemed to allude to this, although Holmes told me that wasn't what it referred to at all.

"There is indeed a royal connection, but it is between them all," he said.

One afternoon, as we made our way to the house of a client, a wild-eyed man collared Holmes on the street, shouting wild accusations.

"It's the 'ace detective', Mister Sherlock Holmes! Are you on another dark mission, given to you by John?"

Holmes eyed me with a dark glint. This was the first time I had been included in a conspiracy. Normally I was depicted as an unknowing accomplice.

"Do you mean to suggest the good doctor here is some kind of sinister puppet master?" Holmes asked.

The man stared at me as if I were a woodlouse, then turned back to Holmes.

"No, not him! John Locke, of course!"

This gave us pause.

"John Locke, the Father of Liberalism?" I asked. "He died in 1704…"

"Lies!" he shouted. "He made himself immortal by taking the Tablet Rasa. Now he controls the government and the queen through mystical arts…"

It was evident that this man was mentally unwell so we looked around to see if we could find assistance.

"And now Locke conspires with Kaiser Wilhelm and the Count of St. Germain to… to… oh fiddlesticks, what was the next part?"

At this point to my surprise a young woman stepped out from behind a tree with a script.

"'…to transform all Londoners into marmosets," she recited.

"That was it!" said the now rather eloquent-sounding man, "Terribly sorry chaps, I hope you enjoyed what you heard anyway."

"This is… a street performance?" I asked with incredulity.

"That's right, an excerpt from our new play, *Sherlock Holmes and the John Locke Conspiracy*. Please try and come."

I came to a realization, "So you… don't know who this gentleman is?" I said, pointing at Holmes.

The actor peered at him, "Should I?"

Holmes remained impassive as I inquired, "What would you do if he was the real Sherlock Holmes?"

The actor puffed out his cheeks thoughtfully, "My goodness, I'd be terribly embarrassed, I think! Can you imagine if that happened?"

The two players wandered off in search of their next victims, "You didn't even crack a smile, Holmes," I said.

"I was working on what the Americans call 'my poker face'," said Holmes.

"Wait… marmosets??"

Hints
Royal connection between them all, not just the king and queen.
There's a poker connection.

A BRITISH CLIPPER SHIP

How many triangles are there?

"What is this connection between Moriarty and the maritime?" Holmes declaimed aloud.

We had been sitting in personable silence for three quarters of an hour. He was reading a scientific book about the growing potential of pneumatic technology and I was poring through *The Times,* trying not to notice several promising criminal cases hinted at in the details of mundane-seeming stories. Too much time with Holmes had trained my brain to spot them and it was very distracting.

Holmes had spoken but not yet given an indication if he really sought my input or was simply looking for an opportunity to explain something he had realized.

"Do waterfalls count as maritime?" I asked, trying to derail things somewhat.

"I ask this because I have noted a growing theme in this deck of cards," Holmes said, turning to me with a cunning look in his eye, holding up a card. "For example, this one features a hull of a ship rendered in triangles. When you count them, you must, of course, remember the bigger triangles are composed of smaller ones as well."

"Of course!" I said, trying to scan the card in the few seconds before Holmes whipped it away and lay back in his chair.

"But I had never before made a connection between the Professor and the sea," he continued.

"Of course, the surname Moriarty actually means 'sea worthy' in the Irish language. But people's surnames don't predict their future occupation."

He refilled his pipe thoughtfully, "Although… Holmes *does* come from the middle-English word for island. And I do live on an island, both literally and, sometimes it seems, intellectually."

"And I'm the son of Wat, mighty warlord," I added. "So perhaps I should invade your intellectual island and ask you to stop this speculation and get to the point."

Holmes now turned to face me, seemingly very serious.

"The point is that, if these cards serve only as a device of distraction, the general nautical theme is unimportant. But if they do have greater significance then I need to gather more data if we are to avoid some future incident. Especially considering the contents of card 16."

"You still haven't shown me that card, Holmes…" I said.

"Watson, I trust you inherently. But the information on that card is a burden and the fewer of us carrying it the better."

"So what is your next course of action?" I asked Holmes. "Will you contact the Navy yourself? Start roving around shipyards?"

Holmes shook his head, "Sadly, as this deck still may be some kind of trap, I am loath to dedicate any more resources to it and I will simply have to gather any flotsam and jetsam of information that floats my way. And I'd ask you to do the same."

"You mean, like the fact that the flags on the side-view of the boat are also triangles?" I asked.

"I had already noticed that, thank you dear Doctor. Just keep a weather eye out."

Hints
Bisecting lines don't invalidate bigger triangles.
Some triangles are formed by other triangles combining.

Puzzle 24
HOUNDS

Identify the breeds,
then find the odd one out.

1.
2.
3.
4.
5.

We had not seen Sir Henry Baskerville for several years, not since the events I detailed in *The Hound of the Baskervilles*. So we were interested to hear from Holmes' network of informants that the young lord had been seen in London in the company of some objectionable looking men, in areas with high concentrations of stray dogs. Some even thought he might have captured several dogs using some kind of lure.

After the sinister trick played on him by Jack and Beryl Stapleton, I wondered if the previously kind and thoughtful young man might have become fixated on some kind of revenge on the whole species, or was possibly even securing them for some kind of dog-baiting ring.

When Holmes suggested I meet him in Battersea at 8pm, I was concerned.

I exited the carriage to find Holmes on the corner, looking around sharply.

"What now, Holmes?" I asked. "A place of concealment? Some kind of disguise?"

"No, now we look at this card," he said, pulling it out of his pocket and showing me five pictures of canines. He had promised that the cards would not disrupt any serious or dangerous business so I was somewhat put out by him taking time to explain that chow chow dogs have small pointed ears, and basset hounds are notable for their long ears and short legs.

"I already know this Holmes, the supposed ghostly hound was a basset! Are we tracking Sir Henry?"

"No, we are meeting him. Here."

We entered a nearby building and the sound and scent of many dogs was suddenly strong around me, accompanied, surprisingly, by the sound of cats. But the people inside the entrance didn't look like hardened criminals but instead a group of average citizens, smiling as we moved through.

Holmes didn't seem surprised by the ranks of dogs in cages, many of which seemed to be surprisingly content and well looked after. We saw Sir Henry at a table with a fierce-looking older woman, washing a mongrel in a tin bath, which was writhing not out of aggression but at unfamiliarity with the procedure. He spotted us and smiled broadly.

"Gentlemen, glad you could come! Welcome to Battersea Dogs Home."

I felt foolish as Sir Henry detailed how, after the abuses Jack Stapleton had inflicted on the basset he had used to create the false ghostly hound, he had become increasingly interested in canine welfare.

"My wife was concerned I would turn Baskerville Hall into a new shelter for strays! I had no such plan but I teased her about it for a few days, making barking noises round the corner."

"So instead you are working here?" I suggested.

"I started just by donating money but I find assisting them more satisfying."

I felt bad for thinking the worst and shook his hand but declined to adopt any of the occupants.

"Possibly wise, Watson, as your eye for a good dog is a little lacking. In fact, one of the pictures on this card isn't of a dog at all…"

Hints
Chow chows have little pointy ears, basset hounds have big ears and short legs.
One of the dogs is not a dog at all.

Puzzle 25

BLACKMAILER'S SAFE

How many turns are needed, for each dial, to reach the combination below?

Remember you have to turn each dial 90 degrees counterclockwise each time.

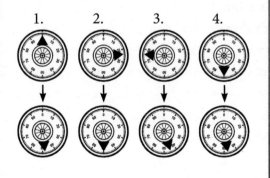

I have often seen Holmes reject a case. But I have not often seen him resolve to destroy the man who tried to hire him. This happened after an anonymous individual sent a letter to Holmes seeking to employ him, asking for personal details of several of Holmes' clients and for him to investigate several others.

"He suggested I could join his... 'payroll'," said Holmes with great venom as he recounted the events. "He thinks only about money. I suspect this is a particular blackmailer who has recently plagued our city. I don't doubt he has a safe filled with people's secrets, accessible with a simple, 90-degree turn of a dial. To evade my capture is infuriating, but to deliberately try to corrupt me..."

I had never seen such rage in Holmes' eyes.

"You have no inkling of his identity?" Watson asked.

Holmes pursed his lips, "I have some ideas. I may be able to drive him out into the open, but of course that doesn't mean he'll face justice as his victims will not seek recompense. We can only hope that one day he crosses the wrong person."

"Surely he's already done that by messaging you?" I said.

"What I mean, Watson, is while he may keep the secrets locked in his safe, accessed by turning every dial, he cannot keep himself there, and some things cannot be deflected with money. Like a bullet."

Of course, the man was Charles Augustus Milverton, and Holmes was later proved correct...

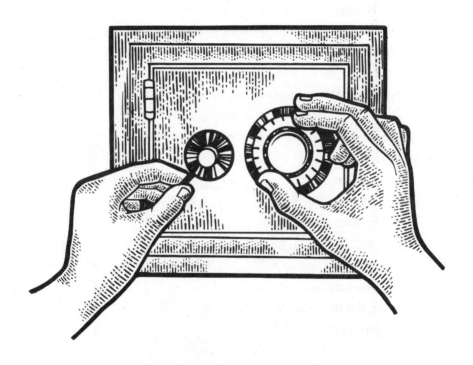

Hints
Each turn is 90 degrees.
You MUST turn every dial.

ROGUE'S GALLERY

Match a) the Thug, b) the Baby Farmer,
c) the Cutpurse and d) the Grandee

The Grandee is wearing a black hat.
The Cutpurse has a moustache only.
The Farmer is facing forward.
The Thug is wearing a bowtie.

1.

2.

3.

4.

Holmes had tickets to see a new production of *Der Freischütz* at the Royal Opera House in Covent Garden. However some technical problems had delayed the commencement of the opera and Holmes had become restless as we sat in the box waiting. He was assessing the other patrons.

"Some of them we know, of course. Lord Marsdon, Donald Featherstonehaugh, Phyllida Bron in the opposite box. However, here's a challenge for you Watson: which of the people in the box directly opposite has recently committed a crime?"

I wasn't sure if he was being honest so I peered across at the box that faced ours. Four people occupied it, looking similarly bored. Holmes began describing the person he meant, but only in relation to ways they were like and unlike the other occupants, and I began to get lost.

"It's simple Watson, take my notepad and draw up a grid, then you can simply mark those who do and don't share characteristics and then eliminate them one by one!"

I did as he asked, and as he described various details like hats, collar lengths etc, I managed to single it down to a strikingly red-haired woman.

"Correct Watson, but what is her crime?"

I thought carefully about crimes that women commit. "Baby farmer?" I joked.

"No, she has no ticket for that box. Her evident excitement practically screams it."

"Shall we report her, Holmes?"

Holmes shook his head, "Let us leave the drama for the stage."

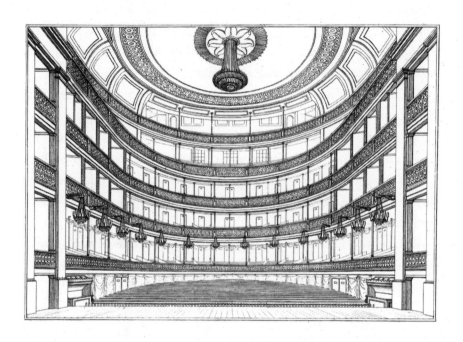

Hints
You can make a grid and use it to eliminate possibilities.
Baby farmers tend to be women.

Puzzle 27

THE QUEEN'S HOUSE

Only one of these statements can be true.

Which, and where is the Queen residing?

1. The Queen is in residence here.

2. The Queen is not in residence here.

3. The Queen is not in residence in House 1.

4. The Queen is in residence in House 3.

Σ

We stood within the horseshoe cloister of Windsor Castle and Holmes was annoyed.

Consulting on security arrangements bores him intensely.

"My mind needs riddles to untangle," he grumbled, "not to look at the rotas of guardsmen."

But he could not refuse this particular request as it came from the Royal Household. The recent assassination of President Carnot in France had concerned those tasked with protecting Her Majesty, and so they had reached out to Holmes in the hope that he could help them see if there were any cracks in their security, through which an anarchist or anti-monarchist might squeeze.

As it happened, Holmes felt that their security measures were largely sound. At one point they had thought he was concerned about access through the Norman Gate but instead he removed a card from his pocket and remarked that, "The solution requires choosing each statement in turn and remembering to reverse the other statements' intentions to see if they are possible." The guards all wrote this down.

At the end of the day Holmes had identified a few blind spots and areas of ingress they had missed and they were extremely grateful.

"I think the greatest danger to Her Majesty is not a lone anarchist infiltrating the castle, but the numerous steep staircases and sub-standard heating," he remarked as we left. "In truth she has so many residences, it would be difficult to know when and where to strike. She cannot be in Osborne House and Windsor Castle at the same time…"

Hints

*Go through each statement, and turn every other statement into
its opposite to see if it can be true.
House one's statement definitely can't be correct as that would
mean two's statement would be true as well.*

COMMON BIRDS OF THE UK

Identify the birds.

1.

2.

3.

4.

5.

W e squatted in the hunting hide on the edges of the Swithenbank Estate in Yorkshire, on a bright and unusually chilly May morning. We were waiting to see if Sir Theodore Swithenbank's former Head Groom, Robert Oates, was hiding out in the nearby woods. Sir Swithenbank had hired Holmes to ascertain what was afflicting his horses, and Holmes had decided that Oates had not, in fact, gone abroad but was concealed in the Estate's forest, emerging in secret to poison his former charges. Swithenbank refused to believe his loyal Groom could be responsible.

Our tense but quiet vigil was broken by the sudden arrival of a keen looking young man, bearing several large cases.

"Hullo, I wasn't expecting there to be a crowd!" he exclaimed as he entered the hide and began unpacking a camera. "I was worried you might be here to hunt birds, but I can see you don't have any guns," he said, grinning.

"We're just here to watch," I said quickly, dropping my voice down to a whisper in response to an acidly raised eyebrow from Holmes. The young man got the hint and lowered his voice too.

"Really? Excellent! I'm Cherry Kearton. I've been taking some pictures hereabouts. Got a wonderful shot of a magpie taking wing a few days ago, great clarity on the white feathers. I'm looking to get one of the brace of local ravens over there, thought I got one yesterday but it was too small, probably another rook."

Holmes now fixed Kearton with a kindly but penetrating stare.

"The truth is that we are not watching for birds but for another more dangerous animal, whose flight at this time would be a great shame for Sir Swithenbank."

"A man?" Kearton said, with disbelief.

"A horse poisoner," I added seriously.

Our animal-loving friend, understanding the task, immediately fell into silence. Within 20 minutes we saw a man emerge from the woods, bedraggled and beetle-browed, and carrying a shotgun like it was his own child. Holmes whispered to me sharply.

"That's the devil. However I think apprehension will be impossible at this point. The visibility today is so high he'll spot our approach with well enough time to bag at least one of us with that Browning."

"Well, at least we can confirm to Swithenbank the truth of your suspicions," I whispered back.

"I fear our word will not be enough for the fellow," said Holmes.

"Hold on…" said Kearton, and he activated his camera. "Once I get this back to my dark room, perhaps you'll have visual proof. The light seems well today so chances are good."

Holmes nodded with satisfaction, giving Kearton a look of respect.

"Perhaps you are right. Thank you."

"I just want to help people appreciate nature," Kearton said with passion. "We're all part of the same taxonomy. Crows, ravens, and jackdaws are all the same family, same genus, but with many interesting differences. Humans are the same."

Hints
Ravens are bigger than rooks, magpies have white feathers.
Some birds are part of the same "family" (corvidae).

OMNE IGNOTUM
PRO MAGNIFICO

"From this man's appearance I observe: a) he was in a rush this morning, b) he anticipated falling asleep while on his journey, c) he originates from Germany, d) he had a typically brutal upper class schooling and e) the train broke down and he was forced to walk to the nearest station. What elements indicate this?"

"I sense Moriarty might be mocking me with this one, Watson," said Holmes, brandishing a particular card at me.

Lestrade had called us in on what he felt was a particularly fiendish mystery involving a broken tree branch, but Holmes had solved it within minutes and was now expressing his boredom by openly going through the deck of puzzles while at the 'crime scene'. Lestrade was pursing his lips in irritation but chose not to say anything.

I looked at the card in question and it did indeed seem to be a jab at Holmes' deduction style.

"He's got your trick down pat Mr. Holmes, no question," said Lestrade, peering over my shoulder.

"It isn't a trick, Lestrade," said Holmes, bristling somewhat. "Merely a method by which I can provide my bonafides to assuage any dubiousness regarding my skills. A time-saving measure."

Lestrade chuckled at this, "And the self-glorification that comes from it is merely a happy by-product, I assume."

"His deductions here are painfully simplistic," Holmes continued, ignoring Lestrade. "Almost everyone knows that the German upper-class are always schooled in fencing, from the moment they can lift a sword..."

"Looking at people and figuring things out about them is not a special skill," said Lestrade plainly. "It's the manner in which you do it, like a magic trick, that rankles some folk."

Lestrade now turned to look at a woman walking up the street towards us, a stranger by all accounts.

"I deduce..." he began, "that this young lady walking up the street is of noble-birth but works for charity. Despite the seemingly shabby nature of her clothes, she moves with the swift, steady stride of the higher-born. Also she has a poise and grace that several years at finishing school..."

But he was unable to finish his sentence because the young lady charged up to him and began screaming in his face.

"You're that little rat what closed my pie shop last week!" she shouted. "All of Stepney was laughing at us! How was I supposed to know where that beef come from?"

"Um… Madam…" Lestrade muttered, but she continued shouting in the same vein for a minute or two before a couple of constables took pity on their boss and escorted her away. Holmes, to his credit, was trying not to laugh, as was I, and neither of us were doing a good job of it.

Holmes stepped forward and laid his hand on Lestrade's shoulder.

"Listen, my brother Mycroft outpaces my deductive reasoning. He would have looked at this card and immediately identified the man's hat as the traditional German Homburg, unconventional on these shores. But he does not trouble himself to leave his chair to confirm any single one of his thoughts."

Lestrade looked slightly mollified as Holmes continued.

"Whereas you, my friend, are so dogged and determined that you don't need these… tricks. You go right up to the door of knowledge and batter it down!"

I could not disagree with that.

Hints
German upper-class schooling usually involved fencing lessons.
Homburgs weren't common in the UK in 1891.

Puzzle 30
WORLD

Holmes read the newspaper headline, "'Dorrington and Hicks solve the Sidcup heist!' Such rot, Watson. Horace Dorrington is a blackguard of the worst water."

"And Hicks?"

"A mere space filler. I fear your stories have led to a hunger for similar tales and now charlatans are being elevated to the level of..."

"You?" I asked pointedly.

"...Us," Holmes finished. "Most of these stories feature a duo, so as to serve as a tonic, both to the reader's sense of justice and of camaraderie. Carnacki and Dodgson, Lady Molly and Mary..."

"Burke and Hare?" I suggested.

"Not the type of 'adventure' I was thinking of, thank you Watson. But see, it must always be two: a match!"

"Do you resent that I have nudged myself into the limelight, Holmes?" I asked.

"No, the opposite is true. I feel that this fixation on only two people leaves out the many others who make this work possible. I will admit my ego appreciates recognition, Watson, but the work of the police, my irregulars, Mrs. Hudson, for goodness sake!"

"This is surprisingly generous of you, Holmes!" I roared.

"Not generosity but practicality, Watson. If these people continue to be underappreciated, their enthusiasm will wither and resentment gather. Like the minute hand of a clock, these affronts accumulate, and what it points to..."

And then Holmes suddenly reached into his pocket and pulled out one of the cards in a frenzy of realization.

Hints
Combine with clock card.
Where the minute hand points is the country you seek.

Match the plant to the poison
it produces.
Which is non-poisonous?

A. Digitalis   B. Solanine
C. Cascabela   D. Nicotine
E. Taxine

1.

2.

3.

4.

5.

6.

I have visited the famous Kew Botanical Gardens several times, but it was only when I went there with Holmes that I discovered it had its own special police force.

"Their jurisdiction only occurs within the park, so they exercise their power over their small fiefdom with fierce pride, Watson," he said, as we strolled across one of the manicured lawns, smoking one of his damnable pipes with such ferocity I was reminded that nicotine is not only addictive but even deadly in large enough quantities.

When we met Constable Unsworth, he had a sharply pressed, spotless uniform and an attitude to match.

"When we received notification of your visitation we immediately swept into action, Mr. Holmes," Unsworth said, more in the manner of my old army commander than a policeman. "We have gathered and assessed our resources and are ready to perform a sweep of the park…"

"I'm just here to visit the Temperate House, Constable. I am not on a case, although I'll inform you if that changes…"

The man looked so disappointed that Holmes asked him to ascertain whether or not someone had tampered with the marigolds outside the Waterlily House.

"Of course, Sir!" Unsworth practically shouted. "You know in India they use them in their wedding ceremonies. I served out there for five years!"

My suspicions of his background confirmed, Holmes and I enjoyed a leisurely afternoon while Unsworth interrogated some flora.

Hints
Nicotine is not only highly addictive but can be deadly too.
Marigolds play a big part in Indian weddings.

Puzzle 32
THE DANCING BEAR

Escape. Only music soothes the bear. It takes 20 seconds to wake or snap out of its reverie. Which boxes do you need to wind in which order to have time to pick the lock? You cannot do two and three simultaneously.

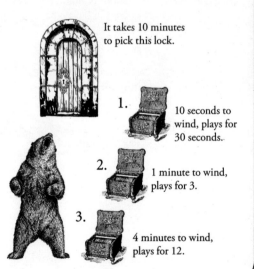

It takes 10 minutes to pick this lock.

1. 10 seconds to wind, plays for 30 seconds.

2. 1 minute to wind, plays for 3.

3. 4 minutes to wind, plays for 12.

The tobacconist who mixed Holmes' particular blend of pipe tobacco had recently been unwell, unable to sleep at night due to "frenzied nighttime violin playing".

The other occupants of his boarding house confirmed this: at midnight a shrieking, unending violin noise would begin, and not stop until 7am. They had searched every room and some of the wall cavities, but to no avail. The violin's noise echoed around the old building's halls so much that they said it was impossible to pinpoint its source. We went to the boarding house, located near Fleet Street.

"It is the ghost of Professor Shrenker!" howled a lady of advanced years, gripping an already sodden handkerchief. "The other people here hounded him out for his eccentricities! He has not been seen since he was evicted, and they found his scarf in a sewer grate…"

She dissolved into sobs, cradling a music box the professor had given her. She let it play through, rewinding it repeatedly, and Holmes seemed to take note of this.

The other residents disputed her interpretation but agreed that the professor had left before the noise had started, though he was not known to play the violin.

After these conversations, Holmes suggested that we return at midnight.

When we came back, we were unsurprised to find all the house's occupants waiting for us, like a small audience, looking very hopeful, especially poor old Mr. Balaskas, Holmes' tobacconist. At the stroke of midnight we heard a strange clicking straining noise, and then the violin began, screeching as loudly and atonally as the people had promised. I could see why sleep was impossible.

Holmes put his hand on the wall then turned to the group's unofficial leader, a stout little man named Potts, "Did you search the basement?"

"Yessir, we did, nothing down there but old broken furniture and damp."

"Damp, of course!"

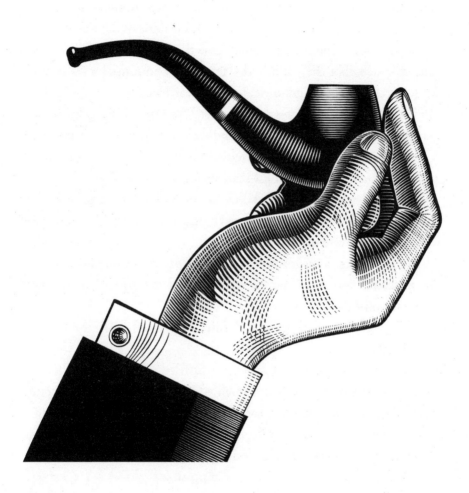

The Dancing Bear

Holmes dashed to the basement, and I could barely follow him for the crowd of rushing residents.

When he arrived down there, he began merrily pulling back soiled divans and split chairs until he found, under a mildewed rug, a stone trapdoor! He lifted it with effort and the violin sound was suddenly five times as loud!

Holmes leapt down and a few brave souls followed him, and we saw something remarkable: a large clockwork machine with a violin fixed at the middle. As the coil unwound, a mechanical arm drew the bow across it. Holmes reached forward and plucked it from the arm, ending the noise. It was inside a very small tunnel filled with thigh-deep water, which turned a strangely shaped metal mill-wheel…

"Incredible," said Holmes with wonder, "a giant music box. See, this water winds it, and when the spring is tight, it begins playing, every midnight! Professor Shrenker's revenge, I suspect."

The water, we learned later, was diverted from the underground Fleet river. The professor was never found but the device was carefully removed and is in the collection of the Science Museum, but only partially wound.

Hints
You will need to wind boxes more than once.
You can wind boxes part of the way.

Puzzle 33

A PECULIAR FILING SYSTEM

What is the next number
in this filing system?

2

6

38

1446

?

One of Holmes' Baker Street Irregulars gave me a message indicating that I should join Holmes at the London Library in St. James' Square.

I arrived outside the London Library at 2pm and was swiftly ushered inside by a friendly librarian. Holmes had been gifted a membership after helping the current administration uncover a book smuggling ring within their ranks.

Holmes sat at a desk in the primary reading room, poring over a history of clothes cleaning and maintenance from the 12th century. He smiled and indicated the seat next to his, and then said no more, continuing to read.

"Why have you…" I began, but Holmes put his finger to his lips, inclining his head towardss a large gentleman in the corner who was working his way through a particularly substantial tome.

Holmes quickly wrote something in his notebook and passed it to me. In his distinctive scrawl, I read:

"Researching use of laundries as way to fraudulently conceal stolen funds. Solved new card."

He turned the page to show he had inserted one of the cards between the pages. It showed a row of books with a series of numbers on them, inviting the reader to calculate the final missing number.

Holmes scrawled in his book again. "Multiplication is the key here."

I gestured towardss the notebook and Holmes permitted me to write "Is that only reason why you called me here?"

Holmes shook his head and wrote further.

"Man in corner is embezzler. Taken £5,000 from job as charity treasurer. Was in hiding but he loves books. I lured him out with false suggestion that the manuscript he's reading has way to avoid jail for crimes."

"You want me to contact police?" I wrote.

"No hurry," Holmes wrote. "Research proving fruitful. Embezzler is huge coward and will come quietly."

During this time I had been staring at the card and finding myself unable to calculate the final number. I passed it to Holmes, shrugging.

Holmes mimed something with his hands that resembled someone wearing boxing gloves trying to play Thimblerig. When he saw I couldn't follow, he took his notebook back and wrote in it once more.

"What to multiply numbers by? Not each other. Or any other number. Only one other option. Then addition is required. Same number for each. Once you solve that you have final number. Not viable filing system but passable puzzle."

I tried to do as he said, but the man in the corner had opened a satchel at his feet and pulled out what appeared to be a loaded shotgun.

"Ah," said Holmes out loud, "it seems our friend may not be as cowardly as I thought." And we both prepared for a dangerous encounter.

The London Library was extensively renovated two years later, and the real reason was never revealed to the public, but those who had the capacity to recognize shotgun damage probably had a good idea!

Hints

It involves multiplication.
You have to multiply the numbers by themselves and add a certain number.

Puzzle 34
MATCH

The player passed seven men
and scored, and at that minute they
knew what country he came from.

I had become increasingly keen on association football, after a friend of mine had joined a well-regarded team, and I had supported him at many matches. Holmes had expressed no interest whatsoever, being principally concerned only with the sport of justice, but on the occasions when my enthusiasm overwhelmed me, and I found myself compelled to try to describe the events of a match to him, he was at least patient enough not to visibly yawn or simply leave the room.

Therefore I was surprised when he asked to attend a match with me, between my friend's team Clapham Rovers and Old Carthusians FC. I felt it most likely that Holmes was either in pursuit of a football fancying criminal or was writing some new analysis of boot-prints or the dirt in fields that required observation of the match.

Instead I found that he was largely watching the game itself rather than anything else, and I wondered if he simply wished to enjoy the match, but then I noticed he was occasionally glancing at another of those infernal cards.

"Is that why you came, Holmes?" I asked, not unkindly.

"This card has a football-related riddle and for the deuce of me I cannot seem to solve it! I thought perhaps attending an actual match might give me some insight but it remains mysterious."

"Oi, mate, where'd you get that card?" said a nearby fan. "Cigarette packet?"

"They don't do football cards," said another man. "They should though!"

"I must admit, I didn't think it was simply for companionship," I continued to Holmes. "I imagine my readers would be surprised to see the two of us here."

"Yes… two of us… a pair," said Holmes, briefly entertaining a thought before dismissing it when my friend, a forward wearing the number nine, scored a particularly deft goal at the 43rd minute, carefully but firmly barging the goalkeeper in the net. Holmes did not cheer but I could see he had some appreciation of the skill involved.

The match continued in a more moderate fashion with no side gaining particular ground over the other and I could see Holmes' attention waver back to the card. If the deck truly was Moriarty's way of distracting Holmes, he would be disappointed to learn (if he indeed was still alive) that all he was distracting him from was a football game he would never have attended anyway.

The match ended at 1-0 and, as the teams all shook hands in a comradely way, the fans began to filter out of the stands.

"The way Rainham was going in the second half, I reckoned there'd be more goals," said one young lad. "The score should have been, like, 20!"

"20 is a score," said Holmes, thoughtfully. But he still did not solve the puzzle, and you will soon understand why.

Hints
This card needs to be combined with card 30.
A score is 20.

APICULTURE

Find the value of each to solve the final calculation.

= 20

= 24

= 13

= ?

It was characteristic of Sherlock Holmes that, after receiving a knife wound that – had it been a few inches lower – might have been fatal, his primary thoughts were admiration of the weapon.

"A remarkable little blade, Watson," he pondered, as I cleaned the area and applied bandages. "Made of glass. In fact, some believe a glass knife can hold a much sharper edge than a metal one."

"Bill Banks didn't seem the type to have an interest in exotic knifeware," I remarked. "He seems more like someone who would blackjack a man and then kick him in the ribs."

"Yes, I suspect he has stolen this from someone else. Such a neat little thing, like the sting of a bee."

I groaned inwardly as somehow Holmes had brought the subject round to bees again, a recent fixation of his that I did not share.

"Or like the claw of a tiger?" I ventured, trying to dodge more bee talk, but Holmes suddenly reached into his pocket and produced the deck of cards.

"A few inches higher and Bill Banks might have skewered the deck," he said, flipping through to find a card with bee pictures on it. "Ah, of course, the worker bee represents the number 10!"

"Are you not at all concerned with your physical safety?" I asked.

Holmes now shared with me a look of utter sincerity.

"Watson, don't fret. My mind may stagnate at inactivity but that does not mean it views my body as an inexhaustible machine. I know I can't survive being stabbed every Tuesday. I shall retire one day. And perhaps keep bees. Their multiplication fascinates me."

Somehow I found the prospect of Holmes retiring more unthinkable than him dying.

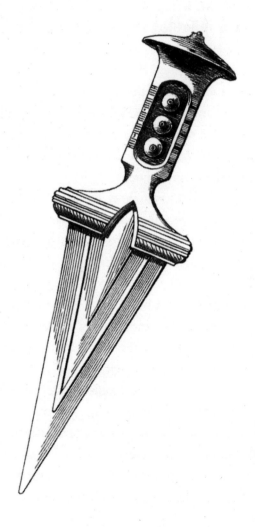

Hints
Worker bees = 10.
The last sum requires multiplication as well as addition.

Puzzle 36

A DROP OF
THAMES WATER

There is more than just bacteria lurking
in this drop of Thames water.

It was Dr. Elizabeth Carlton-Rose's chance to be surprised, I thought, as we knocked on the door of her laboratory. Not the one inside the Natural History Museum, where we made our previous acquaintance, but her secondary, apparently secret one, located in a disused warehouse in Stepney.

Holmes had been gathering information for weeks, and the surprisingly mobile doctor had been seen in many parts of the city, always ostensibly there in service of the science of pneumatics. By analyzing her movements, Holmes had been able to suppose that she had a secondary place of research.

She opened the door to us, and for a moment genuine shock appeared on her face but she tamped it down and invited us inside without a single word of protest.

"Make yourself comfortable. I think I have a teapot somewhere around here..." she said, wandering off, though pointedly staying within eye-range.

Holmes moved toward a microscope on the table and peered through it. "Bacteria?" he asked meaningfully.

"That's a little question, Mr. Holmes," she said, brandishing a very chipped-looking china teapot. "And the answers are hidden very small. Bacteria affects the art of pneumatics considerably, because, if the air that passes through is contaminated, it will pose a risk to anyone who uses the machinery..."

"Come, madam, be honest!" I said, annoyed at the continued coyness. "You are not simply a lady scientist but some manner of..."

And then I stopped, because I honestly did not know what she truly was.

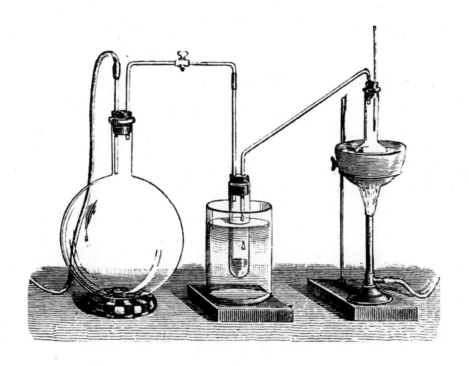

Hints
A little question.
The answers are hidden very small.

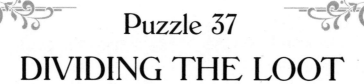

Puzzle 37
DIVIDING THE LOOT

Can you connect all of these valuable
items, matching like with like, with just
three lines?
You cannot go through any of them
or outside the square, and the lines
cannot cross.

When we arrived at Grimwood's auction house, the auctioneer, a Mr. James Downing, was agitated.

"It isn't that any items are missing. The opposite is true! An item has appeared and we do not know its origin! Not only that, but it suddenly also has an entry in our catalogue!"

He turned and indicated the item in question: a bronze figurine of a lion in repose.

"It is German, early 17th century. No sign of it being a forgery."

Holmes peered at the lion with his magnifying glass. "And you are sure that it's not a simple oversight of someone forgetting it had been delivered?"

"No, in fact we have questioned every other worker here and they also have no record of its existence."

Holmes raised an eyebrow.

"So why did you contact me directly, instead of the police?"

The auctioneer looked sheepish. "We're not sure if a crime has been committed. And we'd rather keep this secret. If people thought our security was compromised, it would destroy our business!"

I had thought the guards on the door seemed pretty formidable.

"In fact, Mr. Holmes," he continued, "Could you take it to your residence? Its presence is unsettling the other employees and I am concerned any visitors who see it will wonder about its origins as well."

Holmes paused for a moment. He looked around the room, carefully assessing its contents and the few other auction house workers who were milling around nearby. He pulled the deck of cards out and studied one. "No straight lines..." he muttered. He then gave me a mischievous look and barked out a sharp laugh.

"Incredible! I cannot say that I fell for it for a minute, but I applaud your bravery."

The auctioneer looked confused, a bead of sweat running down his brow.

"Mr. Holmes?"

"I won't be taking the lion, Mr. Downing. Particularly because your name is actually Frank Welborn. Cutpurse, burglar and professional thief."

The auctioneer's body language changed, became hostile, his mouth twisting into a bitter smirk. I glanced around at the other employees, who began to surround us. But in a flash Holmes extracted from his pocket a whistle, and a single piercing blast brought the burly guards into the room to overpower the criminals.

"When I first entered your establishment, I knew you were lying. You were as transparent as tracing paper, which would be useful for solving this card. But to overpower and replace the entire staff of an auction house without alerting the door guards, then try to use *me* as a Trojan horse to remove this valuable item… it's incredible!"

"Where are the actual staff?" I asked.

"Tied up in the stock room," Welborn hissed, struggling in the grip of a guard. "We could have nicked everything if we wanted! We was trying to avoid violence."

"But you decided to bring Sherlock Holmes here? Surely any other detective would have been less likely to spot your game!" I said.

"Watson, please, my blushes."

Welborn rolled his eyes. "We needed Holmes. We come up with the plan quickly and we needed someone… Where we knew where they lived!"

Holmes rolled his eyes, "Ah. Another drawback of having a famous address…"

Hint
The lines don't need to be straight.

Puzzle 38
PIE CHART

Murders committed by my chief assassins in 1889. Moran (1) got the most, the Bone Picker (2) got twice as many as Mistress Stiletto (3), but half as many as Fred Porlock (4). Which assassin corresponds with which piece of the pie?

1.　2.　3.　4.

We were leaving 221B Baker Street to go to lunch when we were stopped suddenly in the street by a formidable looking woman in an enormous bonnet.

"Well, where's the bakery then?" she asked sharply.

"…Which bakers, madam?" I asked, somewhat taken aback.

The woman pointed at the street sign, "The Baker Street Bakery!"

I began to understand, "Madam, simply because this road is called Baker Street does not mean there is a bakery here…"

"As a matter of fact the street was named after William Baker, the architect…" commented Holmes, then he suddenly removed the deck of cards from his pocket and examined a particular one. "Ah yes, Moran is the biggest slice…" he muttered to himself.

The woman's face was now a dark crimson, and I stepped back.

"Don't take me for a simpleton!" she demanded. "I didn't come all the way to London to be told there's no bakery on Baker Street! My good friend Felicity Trubshaw said they have the finest buns in England!"

"Porlock is the next biggest, of course…" Holmes continued, so I was forced to explain, at length and with much hostile interruption, that there was no bakery here and never had been, but that Spikings and co. on Dover Street was a fine establishment.

When she finally believed me, her face returned to its normal shade, and she uttered a half-hearted apology.

"Thank you. I'll go there once I get back from the circus in Piccadilly."

Hints
Moran must be the biggest slice.
Porlock must be the next biggest.

HIGH STAKES

1. Basil's Boy: 38mph, until halfway down to 30mph.

2. Jeremy's Hare: 33mph then up to 35 for last 100 yards.

3. Benedictine: 40mph, collapsed after 1,500 yards.

4. Mickelwhite: 32mph, steadily.

5. Silver Blaze: started at 30 mph, after 50 yards went up to 39mph.

The same 1-mile race, there are 1,760 yards in a mile. WHO WINS?

"Sorry to be bringing you in on another equestrian mystery," said Inspector Gregory, as he sat in the chair opposite Holmes in the study. "You'll think I'm horse mad! Though in truth the mystery doesn't concern horses as much as people."

Hovering on Gregory's left side was Ethel Brown.

"She says she has been slandered. Her husband Robert is a horse-breeder. A stable owner, Elijah Bottle, yesterday claimed he was having an affair with her."

"It's not true! I am a good Christian woman!" Mrs. Brown exclaimed.

"Bottle was seen leaving the Brown household late at night," Gregory explained, "both Mr. Brown and Bottle are currently in custody after a bout of fisticuffs in the yard of Bottle's stables. Maybe he was engaged in burglary, but not a single item is out of place in their house. I wouldn't get you involved but Bottle owns a racehorse named Johnny the Miller, and it's supposed to be running in the Derby Stakes at Epsom next week!"

"Is that correct?" said Holmes, pulling a card from his pocket and studying it. "Benedictine did not finish, that much is certain," he muttered, before pocketing it and standing up. "Take me to the Brown household."

The inside of the Browns' house was tidy and clean (though it smelled strongly of horses from the adjoining stable) and any out-of-place detail would surely have been detected. Holmes carefully inspected the door through which Bottle was seen leaving.

"The only thing I found even remotely odd was a very small quantity of grease here on the edge of this table," said Gregory. "But Mrs. Brown said it could have been from…"

Holmes held up his hand, "Excellent data gathering, Inspector. Mrs. Brown, where does your husband keep his studbook?"

"In the bureau drawer, sir."

Holmes went to open it.

"Careful sir, it sometimes sticks," she said, but as Holmes opened

it with one smooth motion, they both got an inkling of what had occurred. Holmes took out the studbook, a breeding register, and turned to a particular page.

"A-ha! To the untrained eye this tome indicates that 'Johnny the Miller' was born in 1891. But it was originally 1890, it has been altered with a modicum of skill."

Bottle was confronted with this evidence and the truth came out. He'd received pressure to enter Johnny the Miller in the Epsom Derby but the race only permitted three-year old horses, and, as the horse was relatively unknown he thought he could falsify the records without anyone realizing, using the grease to open what he knew was a difficult drawer. Holmes told Bottle that Basil's Boy lost its lead halfway through, and we were all briefly confused until I realized he was reading from the card again.

"To me the greater crime was besmirching the name of my dear wife," said Mr. Brown later, holding her hand and smiling at her fondly.

"I suggest next time you trust your own spouse over the word of a scoundrel," said Inspector Gregory gruffly.

Hints
Benedictine did not finish.
Although Basil's Boy starts very fast, it loses its lead halfway through.

Puzzle 40
PHILATELY

Which is the odd one out?

I do not often have cause to visit the General Post Office in St. Martin's Le Grand but Holmes insisted I should mail a package for him in person.

When I arrived, I found it to be just as cramped, badly lit and malodorous as the legends had it. I made my way through scores of clerks, busily, examining and stamping all sizes and shapes of mail, until I felt a hand on my shoulder and turned to see a pale looking old man with a prodigious twisty beard that contained a few wayward stamps. He held up what I thought at first was a sheet of Penny Blacks but on closer inspection was instead a playing card with an image of Penny Blacks printed upon it.

"Look at this! One of these is worth more than a penny, if ye understand what I mean! Come with me, young man."

Sherlock Holmes (for I had intuited it was he, I am not a complete fool) led me through a network of corridors and rooms until we reached a tiny cramped one, piled with damp boxes and cobwebs, barely big enough for us both.

"Watson, your arrival is perfectly timed," Holmes said, doffing his fake facial hair. "I couldn't stand another minute in this rat's nest of a beard or this anthill of a place. Every single room is filled with busy workers... except for this one."

He began moving the boxes, dismantling a wall.

"They say it's haunted, but that is a carefully crafted lie designed to deflect superstitious workers from the truth..."

When his work was done, I saw a hole had been carefully cut in the wall, and felt cold air coming from the other side. He passed through without hesitation and I followed.

"Do you recall the pneumatic dispatch railroad?" he asked, lifting a nearby lantern and climbing down a ladder. "An underground delivery system between mail offices? The network was abandoned 15 years ago, but when the Postmaster General himself asked me to investigate disappearing mail, I recalled that one of the attempted tunnels was connected to this very branch..."

We reached the bottom of the ladder and I could see the tunnel stretching east to west.

"This is somehow less cramped and more pleasant than the Post Office," Holmes remarked in a whisper.

"At least during my time there, I solved this stamp puzzle. One does not usually expect to see a *Pearly* Queen on a Penny Black…"

Suddenly we heard shouted words in the tunnel ahead. We had been spotted.

"So who is using the tunnels?" I asked, drawing my pistol. "Thieves? Smugglers?"

"Worse," said Holmes. "Postmen. A criminal faction within the employees has created a sideline in hijacking valuable mail for its own enrichment. But you will not need your sidearm."

Suddenly Holmes pulled a nearby lever, activating one of the idle trains, which began trundling forward toward the now frightened-looking conspirators.

"The train itself shall apprehend them. Kindly fetch the police and tell them we have a special delivery…"

Hints
One stamp is worth more than a penny.
Pearly Queen.

Puzzle 41

DENIZENS OF BAKER STREET

Who lives in the four other flats?
The possible occupants are:

Col. Sebastian Moran, master hunter.
Emmanuel Strukov, human taxidermist.
Sir Donald D'eath, stabbing socialite.
Mrs. Hermione Bunn, Droitwich poisoner.

- The second-most dangerous man in London does not live to the right of the ugliest landlady.
- The person with no title lives underneath the person from the Midlands.
- The knight has a wooden leg and chooses to live downstairs.

After our encounter with the nature photographer in Yorkshire, Holmes' interest in the use of a camera as a tool for gathering investigative data had been reignited. It was strangely edifying for me, then, to see a field of study in which Holmes was not already an expert, and he spent much time in a dark room producing poorly lit or ill-focused pictures he had captured during our travails.

One Wednesday I was making my way to 221B when I saw Holmes in conversation with a similarly thin, serious-looking fellow standing by a camera mounted on a tripod out on the street.

"Ah Watson, this gentleman here is attempting to take photographs of Baker Street's buildings," said Holmes briskly. "I was discussing how he manages to compensate for problems such as the light levels and the pedestrians."

"A challenge, certainly," the photographer said in a crisp, dark voice. "I like to pursue various side projects but my trade is in portraits. I even photographed someone of your acquaintance."

"Sebastian Moran," said Holmes.

The photographer seemed very casual about his encounter, taking a picture of the second most dangerous man in London!

"I trust you checked your money was not forged!" I said.

"I don't really take money as my payment," said the photographer, his voice strangely clear over the noise of the crowded street. "I prefer to find individuals with potential and allow them to achieve... exposure."

I found him quite unsettling. "And Moran's potential was to become this city's greatest predator?"

"Second-greatest," said the photographer, almost wistfully, "although you have not recaptured him, I hear."

I didn't care for the tone of the conversation, and I saw Holmes too was a little unsure.

"You work here in the city?" Holmes asked.

"I travel around," the photographer said, adjusting his camera.

"You're as likely to find me in Denmark as Droitwich. I go where I feel talent may lie…"

"Well, perhaps if we are in the North, we shall look in on you," said Holmes with an edge.

"Droitwich is in the Midlands, Mr. Holmes, the locals are very insistent. Perhaps your famed insight has missed that. Nonetheless I doubt someone like yourself needs one of my photographs." He then turned to me.

"You however, Dr. Watson, have decided yourself to be this man's Boswell but without considering your own talents and potential. Perhaps you would like to take my card…"

"No, thank you," I said, with no interest in explaining myself to this suddenly rude fellow.

We excused ourselves and moved toward 221B, Holmes' expression almost unreadably serious.

"A Moriarty minion?" I asked him.

"No, Watson, if I am being truthful, all my instincts and deductions allow me that there is something fundamentally wrong about that man's existence. I doubt I shall ever find any concrete evidence of a crime involving him. I loathe superstition, but it is men like him who help me understand why it exists."

Holmes abandoned his photographic experiments that day and returned to other matters.

Hints
Moran's the second-most dangerous man in London.
Droitwich is in the Midlands.

M

Fill in the blanks.

+		+		+	x
x		−		÷	+
1				3	6
+		x		+	=
			+		20

Σ

Holmes' small band of local urchins and street boys known as the "Baker Street Irregulars" had lamented his apparent death.

Holmes would never admit to being proud of them, but he had privately admitted to me, he had thought they needed his constant influence to remain an "efficient force" and was surprised that during his absence they had not only continued his surveillance and information-gathering tasks but had even formed a small investigative group of their own, with a small number of local successes, mostly regarding stolen goods or preventing intimidation.

Of course, people are less willing to accept help from several young boys caked in dirt with ragged clothes than they are a sharply dressed famous detective, but they did not allow people's negative reactions and suspicion to dissuade them.

Their biggest issue was that Wiggins, the long-time leader of the group, was much more a man than a boy now and could certainly not be described as an urchin. Yet he could not leave behind the sense of purpose he had found within it, even though he was a full foot taller than most of its members.

Holmes was just telling me, "Always divide and multiply before you add and subtract," when Pitt, Wiggins' effective "second in command" and the most likely boy to take over, entered the room and reported that Wiggins had been seen visiting the location of a notorious drug den after hours, without telling the others. None of us looked happy at the implication.

"He told us he was onto getting a delivery job for a newspaper or something but that weren't where he's going. He wouldn't go to the other side, would he, Mr. Holmes?"

Holmes investigated, using what he felt was the most effective technique. He asked Wiggins directly.

"Got the delivery job, Mr. Holmes! But I was thinking whether I could do something else, maybe even write for the paper one day. Given enough tips to journalists in my time. So I been taking writing

lessons with this old teacher what lives in that building, I know there's an opium den there but the old boy ain't got a lot of money himself. He wouldn't be helping me otherwise, would he?"

I was relieved Wiggins hadn't moved into crime because the lad's self-confidence would have made him lord of the London underworld in about two weeks, by my reckoning. I found it hard to believe any newspaper would hire him to write for them with his background, even if Holmes and I put in a good word.

"Wiggins, I trust I shall be seeing your byline in good stead," Holmes said, surprising me. It sounded like a sentiment, not a statement. "But I suggest the Irregulars could help your tutor find alternative accommodation."

"I'm working on that, Mr. Holmes, I'm teaching him some maths so he can get his job back! We're doing Pascal's triangle tonight…"

Hints
Always divide and multiply before you add and subtract.
Pascal's triangle.

FLOORPLAN FOR A ROBBERY

Which entry way will
allow you to access the safe? You may
use more than one.

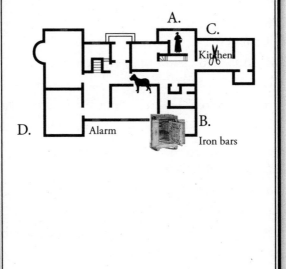

Dr. Carlton-Rose knew that she could no longer claim innocence but she still seemed reluctant to reveal her actual role in the strange series of events we had been thrown into.

"Perhaps I could tell you what I have learned and you can fill in the blanks," Holmes suggested. "You are part of a network of... scientists?"

She nodded, "A multi-disciplinary collaboration, as it were. Primarily female."

"You make it sound rather like a symposium but my investigations suggest you and your colleagues, number unknown, consider yourselves rather more like a force of investigation and justice. I've found countless reports of robberies of scientific institutions mysteriously foiled, malefactors neutralized or simply redirected elsewhere..."

Dr. Carlton-Rose nodded, "We began simply as a method of secretly assisting each other's progress in the face of hostility, both from criminals and from supposed colleagues. Sometimes it was simply a case of having someone in a room we knew would be broken into, so that it did not happen."

"I briefly suspected you to be an agent of Moriarty..." continued Holmes.

"We became aware of Moriarty's network of crime roughly when you did," Dr. Carlton-Rose said, "but our methods are different. We find containment works better than exposure because often we don't trust the mechanisms of justice..."

"That is not your decision to make!" I said. "If you had information you should have passed it on."

She gave me a piercing look. "That's inconsequential, because your friend dismantled a large part of the network and then went for a swim with Moriarty. It is only recently, with Mr. Holmes resurfacing, that we thought..."

"That Moriarty might also have survived?" said Holmes, fiddling with a nearby pneumatic machine. Dr. Carlton-Rose came over and firmly wheeled it out of his grasp.

"No. But when an organization that big breaks up, there's bound to be some flotsam and jetsam. This pack of cards points to something, or somewhere, significant and strange."

"Be that as it may, it's inadvisable for you to continue dogging our footsteps when mad dogs like Sebastian Moran are roving around with loaded weaponry," I said. "I do not say this because you are a woman, madam, but because you are a... civilian."

"I am not dogging anyone's steps! If anything it is you who have been behind mine! But, I admit, you have the deck and therefore the investigative advantage, and so I'll discontinue for a while, but if you feel like you've made headway as to the cards' true meanings, please get in touch and I will help if I can."

"You think we'll need a pneumaticist's advice?" Holmes said tartly.

"I can scale a nine-foot wall in ten seconds, squeeze through a four-foot air duct, and I know where to cut an alarm wire to deactivate it," she said matter-of-factly.

"Because you're a scientist?" I asked.

"Because of women's suffrage, actually. People often tell us to return to the kitchen, but they don't think about how many sharp objects it contains. Now kindly exit my laboratory."

Hints

You shouldn't go into a room where someone is inside.
One of the entrances can be accessed by getting something from the kitchen.

THE BLACK MUSEUM

Match the item to its category.

1) Toxicology
2) Felonious assault
3) Larceny
4) Post-Mortem
5) Fraud

A.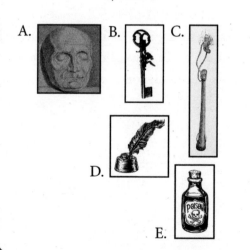

B.

C.

D.

E.

In the early days of their acquaintance Inspector Lestrade had regarded Holmes with dismissive suspicion. But, as time went on, he began to respect Holmes, as he often made Lestrade's job easier than harder. He had mourned Holmes after his apparent death, and heralded his return. So when Lestrade invited us to view Scotland Yard's famous Black Museum, its repository of notable and remarkable evidence from past crimes, we accepted in good faith.

The museum, located in a Scotland Yard basement, was well organized, with a series of glass cases showing the various artefacts. Hangman's nooses, varied melee weapons from 'life preservers' to sword umbrellas, and numerous letters and documents relevant to specific cases.

Holmes had shown no interest in visiting previously. He cared nothing about objects involved in cases, except as sources of data. Holmes valued information more highly, and as the Black Museum had been created to serve as an educational tool for police officers, he approved of its general existence, but he'd had no need to come himself as he did not need to be educated and had even less interest in acting as an educator, unless it was through the writing of monographs.

Nevertheless, he was respectfully attentive as the collection's curator gave a short tour of its items, and even remarked on one of the pieces, a large bronze key formerly possessed by the 18th century forger, John Hatfield, for which they had never found the lock.

"Are you deliberately not mentioning its additional function for a particular reason?" he asked.

"…Additional function?"

Holmes gestured toward the cabinet, "May I?"

The curator unlocked it and passed Holmes the key. Holmes inspected it, twisted the end of the key in an interesting configuration, and then pulled the end away to reveal a hollow compartment within. Lestrade and the curator could not have looked more shocked if Hatfield himself had walked into the room and recovered his property.

"A neat little device. You see the almost imperceptible grooves on its surface?"

"For goodness sake Holmes, what's inside it?" shouted Lestrade, with excitement.

Sherlock tipped the key into his hand and a tiny rolled up parchment landed in it. Conscious that it might be extremely fragile, he carefully unrolled it as the rest of us peered desperately over his shoulder.

"I believe it has the words: 'Grimes Message-Key, the safe and reliable way to hide messages,' printed upon it with India ink." Holmes pointed at a nearby ink bottle in the display case.

We all leaned back, strangely disappointed.

"So I suppose he never used it," said the curator.

"Maybe even *he* didn't know what it was!" said Lestrade, patting Holmes on the shoulder.

Holmes smiled, but then his face dropped when he realized that the curator wanted him to inspect every other item in the collection…

Hints

What looks like a weapon may not be.
Poisoning might need a bottle but forgery needs ink.

Puzzle 45
CONNECTIONS

What connects these images?

1.

2.

3.

4.

5.

"An amusing side effect of your stories, Watson, is that in a strange way they have actually rendered me *less* notable."

Holmes offered me this observation as we walked along Conduit Street, on our way to an important meeting with a young blackmail victim. He briefly looked at one of Moriarty's cards, said "conduits" to himself, then returned to his previous thought.

"Your… embellishments of our experiences, and the rather creative illustrations Mr. Paget provided as an accompaniment, have given the general public a particular idea of what I look like and how I act."

"Do you think my accounts are inaccurate?" I asked.

"One hundred per cent accuracy in anything is impossible! You certainly capture the spirit of our cases. No, what I mean is people expect me to be constantly dashing from place to place, perpetually smoking a pipe and holding a magnifying glass, grimly commanding people from my seven feet of height and saying 'elementary', apparently…"

"I never put elementary in the stories!" I declared.

"I know, and yet somehow it has adhered itself to me. However, what this does mean is that many of these people around us now do not look at me and see 'Sherlock Holmes'. I am in disguise by simply being myself."

"You do smoke a lot though, Holmes, you must admit."

Holmes regarded the pipe in his hand, "Perhaps in your next account you could claim that I have the ability to read men's minds. It would make our work easier."

Hints
Conduits.
Smoking connection.

NITROGLYCERIN PLOT

Nitroglycerin bomb underneath the Houses of Parliament. Perpetrators captured. Only the Bomb Maker can disarm.

- The Bomb Maker does not want to die so will always tell the truth.
- The bomb's Transporter is compelled to always lie.
- The Guard will either tell the truth or lie based on his own interests.
- Who is the Bomb Maker, the Transporter and the Guard?

Holmes paced steadily forward through the basements of the Palace of Westminster, his gas lamp held high, his eyes sharply scanning for anything untoward.

One of the cards in Moriarty's deck had seemed to be blank after he had exposed it to the developing fluid. He was naturally suspicious of this but other treatments proved ineffective at revealing anything further, until he attended a medical lecture with me about the effects of nitroglycerine (called glyceryl trinitrate to avoid alarming patients) on reducing blood pressure.

In the spirit of experimentation, he exposed the card to a sample, then swiftly informed me we must leave immediately and make our way to Westminster with the greatest urgency.

All of the staff, and even a few volunteering MPs, had now taken to searching the premises for a possible bomb. Holmes would have preferred not to involve others due to the risk of a blundering mistake but he had had to explain the circumstances to the authorities to gain entrance as soon as possible and there was no time for nuance.

"It's unlikely Moriarty has planted a bomb here," Holmes admitted. "But if William Parker had dismissed the gunpowder plot as hearsay, we would be living in a rather different Britain today."

Things had changed considerably in the 289 years since the plot, but the Fenian bombs had been only nine years ago so the security forces were at high alert.

"I do wonder if the puzzle contains further clues we could use. SM cannot be the always lying Transporter because he directly says he is the liar. But, other than Sebastian Moran, does SM have a further significance?"

Suddenly a cry went up from part of the building, freezing all inside. "What's this!" was gruffly uttered with a mix of fear and excitement, and the small stampede of individuals toward the room was halted only by Holmes physically standing in their way and explaining the sensitivity of nitroglycerin and bombs in general.

We passed into the side room, used for storage, to find one of the palace's guards quivering as he stood over a large wooden box, inside which was a mass of wires and mechanical parts, all connected together.

"It's the bomb, sir, I'm sure of it!"

Holmes put up a silencing finger and leaned forward carefully.

"My expertise on the construction of explosives devices is limited," he admitted, "but logically this makes no sense. If Moriarty wished to bomb Parliament, why? And a nitroglycerin bomb placed here would have an ineffective blast radius. Perhaps someone was intended to move it…"

Holmes removed a small case from his coat and sprinkled a series of powders onto the device.

"No evidence of the presence of nitroglycerin… but a rather large quantity of arsenic painted onto every component. A fake bomb, but a real trap for you and I, I fear."

The MPs were soon toasting their bravery in the bar, but Holmes and I felt a greater reckoning lay around the corner.

Hints
SM can't be the liar if he says he is.
If MB is the liar, he wouldn't say he's not the guard.

Puzzle 47
DR. JOHN WATSON

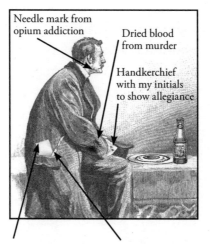

Prove me wrong
−𝓜

Needle mark from opium addiction

Dried blood from murder

Handkerchief with my initials to show allegiance

Bribe money for assassination

Kris in pocket

It was getting to the end of a full day: I had seen a number of patients, met an old friend for lunch, consulted with a colleague about a particular malady that his patient was suffering from, and to my surprise I was able to apply some experience I gained during 'The Adventure of the Beryl Coronet'. I then had a pleasant steak and kidney pie for dinner at home before spending a couple of hours writing down some of my recent experiences with Holmes.

I was just preparing to go to bed when I became aware of a presence in the corner of my room. It was Holmes! He lit a match and put it to his pipe, his manner very casual.

"Watson. Sorry to drop in on you like this. It has become... necessary."

I was tired and, I think, justifiably annoyed at his appearance.

"Holmes, I have got used to some very odd ways in our many experiences together but I do rather think breaking into my house at night is a little beyond the pale. Your expression rather reminds me of that when I saw you several years ago at my practice and you were drawing the blinds to protect against Moran's airgun."

Holmes nodded acknowledgement. "Yes, it is a similar situation, but my concern does not lie with Moran sniping me from a distance..."

He handed me a card from the deck, the final one. It had also been blank, but I could see now an image of myself, covered in cruel slander.

"This one was developed with an antiseptic medical solution, phenol. One you use yourself."

I stared back at Holmes. "Holmes... I think you know me well enough... and I know you well enough... not to believe any of this rot."

Holmes paused for a second, then patted me on the arm with great affection, "I did not doubt you for an instant, Watson. The crude suppositions on this card are all easily disproved and insultingly slow. Dried blood that's bright red? A doctor with a 'deadly knife'. If we arrest all doctors who have knives, we'd have none in public."

He sat in my desk chair.

"No, my seriousness is out of concern for your safety. Moriarty put you here, not to scare me but to threaten me. James Moriarty put the MM handkerchief in your sleeve on the picture to remind me of what you lost, your dear wife Mary…"

"Yes, I realized that. The man is an evil creature, even in death."

"That's the thing Watson, Mary died after Reichenbach Falls. I have solved the strange maritime connection between the cards, and you and I must take a trip right now to resolve this mystery, once and for all."

I had not yet dressed for bed so it was a simple act for me to grab any equipment Holmes suggested, throw on my coat and stride with him out into the moonlight.

STOP

DO NOT GO BEYOND THIS PAGE before you have decided on what you believe is the solution to the clues contained within the cards marked with Moriarty's Σ. The solution is a particular location in London.

Once you have chosen you may turn the page and see if you are correct.

THE CONCLUSION

Many of my adventures with Sherlock Holmes have concluded in strange places at strange times, so when I tell you that I found myself making my way up the hill to Greenwich Royal Observatory at 3am, you may not be surprised.

At first I thought we had a somewhat longer voyage ahead of us. Holmes and I took the fastest possible carriage to St. Katharine Docks, where we dressed in worn but practical outfits and false beards as two rather convincing seamen.

These two bearded seamen then boarded a clipper bound for Australia, the *Cutty Sark*, a 75-day voyage if all went to plan. They were secretively followed by one less convincing sailor, patently Sebastian Moran, bristling with malevolence. He was an excellent shot but a poor impersonator.

We saw all this clearly because the bearded seamen were not us and we were watching from a nearby vantage point, dressed once again in our normal clothes. The people in disguises were two of Holmes' associates, a ruse designed to get Moran off our backs.

"I have asked our friends on the ship to wait a few hours and then seize Moran, perhaps when he's trying to cheat them all at cards. He can then spend the 75 days clapped in irons, thinking about how ill-advised it is to pursue 'vendettas'."

"So Moran truly had no idea of the significance of the cards?"

"I don't doubt Moriarty gave him the pack and solution but no other instructions save that they should fall into my hands somehow.

Now, to the Observatory…"

As we made our way there, Holmes explained.

"All the clues pointed to here, Watson. The Queen's House and the Painted Hall, both here in Greenwich. Clipper ship plans, Lord Nelson and international flags, all maritime connections. Lenses, constellations, time zones, asteroids, an orrery, even a picture of the world with a line across it, like Greenwich's Prime Meridian. The Greenwich Royal Observatory."

We could see it at the top of the hill: an extraordinary construction, a temple to science and reason.

"So what is waiting for us? Is Moriarty going to try to ritually murder you at zero longitude?"

"It's what lies below that interests me… It was Puzzle 46 that brought it together for me. Something built underneath a London landmark by three men called SM, MB and JMc…"

Holmes reminded me of the strange occurrence that March when a French anarchist named Martial Boudin accidentally blew himself up in Greenwich Park. At the time Holmes had been out of the country, pretending to be dead, so he had not had cause to investigate, but no-one was sure why Boudin had done it.

"Martial Boudin or MB was a worker for Moriarty, an expert in underground construction back in France. The Observatory has had some recent renovation and a new telescope installed, but I looked into the building manifests and transportation details and it's all a very clever web of forgeries. There has been a secret construction project here for years, materials being clandestinely shuttled back and forth between the docks and here."

"To what end?"

"I can't be sure until I get there. I spent four nights in a public house near here, disguised as a night soil man, managed to hear a tale from a young sailor named Joseph about a big fight between Boudin and a local eccentric named Jonathan McKenzie, Jock to his very few friends. Much was shouted about money and secrets and 'James is dead!' McKenzie was a construction engineer too, a former navigator turned master builder."

We approached the Observatory's entrance. Holmes had sent a few messages on the way but he had wanted to act as swiftly as possible. Lestrade was rallying the force. But at the moment we were alone.

Suddenly a shot rang out, shattering a tile near Holmes' foot! A shooter on the roof! Was the Moran who went onto the ship a decoy? No, a couple of subsequent shots revealed this gunman had a woeful aim. I pulled out my pistol to effect a return of fire when another shot rang out from behind us, and this had greater accuracy as we heard a deep Scottish voice on the roof swear a litany of oaths as it retreated back inside. I turned to see Dr. Elizabeth Carlton-Rose, bearing a pneumatic rifle that looked several evolutionary steps along from the one Moran menaced Holmes with earlier in the year.

"Head inside, I'll make sure there's no escape this way," she said and I didn't know if I was more surprised at her sudden gunfire or Holmes contacting her. Perhaps he hoped to learn more about her organization based on observing her actions, but critically we needed to go inside.

The Observatory was dark and quiet. Holmes moved past the collections of scientific devices and other evidence of research to the room where the new 28-inch Grubb telescope was in the Equatorial Dome. Holmes moved round to its instruments and adjusted it to point at a seemingly insignificant cluster of stars, and a small panel popped open with four numbered dials. Holmes turned them to 1, 1, 3 and 6 and a trapdoor, unnoticeable by anyone, opened in a small alcove nearby.

We descended some stairs cautiously, the air musty but dry. And then we saw it: a network of rooms, dug into the very earth underneath the Observatory! An initial lobby area, crowned with a huge mosaic Σ, was an ostentatious touch that Holmes scoffed at. I held my pistol and we moved forward, seeing dormitories and laboratories, a cafeteria and an underground garden, but all completely empty, and untouched, as if never used.

As we moved further in, the rooms got larger, but they also got less well built, with organic shapes and in some cases earthen walls, until we were practically walking through caverns.

Something was scrawled on the walls, spiderish marks overlapping. I peered at it.

"Mathematical formulae," I whispered.

"Yes, but even I can see it makes little sense. Mr. McKenzie is not Moriarty."

The tunnel ahead descended into one final grand room, a half-finished crypt covered in the mathematical scrawls which here coalesced into strange, scratchy portraits of Moriarty himself. And in the middle in an enormous, M shaped glass coffin... Moriarty's body!

We paused at the entrance and Holmes raised an eyebrow, "What does this seem like to you?"

"A trap?" I ventured.

Holmes pointed to the side and we attempted to find an alternative way into the room but it seemed the front entrance was the only one. With no alternative, we positioned ourselves either side of the door and dashed inside in opposite directions, and with good reason because McKenzie began taking shots again and in much closer quarters, almost catching us before we found a hiding spot behind some twisted, half-finished columns.

"Welcome, Mr. Sherlock Holmes, to your doom!" boomed the deep voice.

We heard a heavy lever pulled with great effort and a vast metal door slammed down on the entrance, locking us in. Holmes had, of course, already observed it but decided to go inside anyway.

McKenzie now emerged. His enormous, tangled beard was so dirty and matted it looked like a mass of dark tentacles, and he wore a strange, self-made robe covered in his mathematical scrawls.

"I promised the master and provided! A house for him to live underground, in secret and a TOMB for his pathetic parasite!"

He drew his gun level with us, as he scrambled down into the middle of the room and rubbed his hands on the coffin obsessively. His eyes looked like two fried eggs with black yolks.

"It seems it is your master's tomb rather than mine," shouted Holmes.

"Oh no, this isn't him, it can't be, the master is eternal, the navigator god made flesh!"

McKenzie opened the coffin and reached for Moriarty's corpse.

"Martial wanted to leave, take all the money, said the master was dead, who cared," he continued muttering, pulling at Moriarty's burial garments, "threw him out, threw them all out, but he came back for revenge, blew himself up, ha! Idiotic blasphemer…"

He ripped the clothes and even the face off the body, which I could see was a fake, a wooden and rubber dummy, and underneath…

"Had to dig quietly and silently all those years but kept a little bit of this just for you… nitroglycerine!"

The fake body was actually a bomb. A real one this time. And McKenzie had activated it.

"So the deck of cards was meant to get me here?"

McKenzie grinned maniacally.

"Yes, the cards, the trick, the puzzles, to bamboozle you, to tempt you, to confuse and now trap you!"

We had no idea when the bomb would explode but we had to assume it would be soon as it was making alarming noises. I doubted we could convince him to deactivate it.

"We will all become atoms, like planets in an orrery, like stars in the sky. Then the master will return and I will be with him."

Holmes stepped out from behind the column. McKenzie drew the gun level with him but Holmes had correctly guessed that now McKenzie would rather see us all blown up together so he did not shoot him. Holmes removed his own firearm from his pocket slowly and placed it on the ground.

"I enjoyed the deck. Did Moriarty design it?"

McKenzie nodded frantically, "A little game for him, to tease and test you. He had meant to give it to you and watch you chase around before you came here but then he took you to the falls instead. To baptize you!"

"So you haven't seen him since?" Holmes asked cautiously.

"Of course, I have!" McKenzie beamed, "in my dreams, my sweet, sweet day and night dreams."

I leaned forward to try a shot but Holmes gave me a warning look out of the corner of his eye. He edged forward.

"A shame, I had a card I wanted his help with."

McKenzie looked confused and affronted at this, "You… didn't solve all the puzzles? And yet you came here?"

"Unfortunately, yes…" said Holmes, drawing the pack of cards from his pocket.

McKenzie suddenly beamed again, "I can help you!"

"I don't think so," said Holmes. "You are not playing with a full deck."

And he threw the cards in McKenzie's face!

McKenzie reeled back, some of the cards adhering to his beard, and scrabbled for his gun, but I took my chance and shot him straight in the chest. He slumped forward instantly, his blood running into the still-active bomb.

We darted forward and Holmes had to move McKenzie's body aside to regard the bomb. Its workings were too complex to easily discern how to deactivate it and it was shaking with increasing force.

"If we can't turn it off we need to… cool the Nitroglycerin?" I said, thinking how foolish it sounded.

"My thoughts exactly Watson. We have one chance, I think."

Holmes ran to one of the shoddy, wobbly columns.

"Two things I have observed about this room, Watson. One is its inherent structural instability, and the other is the water dripping from the ceiling."

"Which means??" I asked frantically.

"We are under the boating lake," said Holmes, and he shoved the column precisely. A domino effect of poorly constructed crypt architecture smashed one after the other until it breached the thin ceiling and a torrent of water gushed down upon us, flooding the room to neck height! The bomb vanished beneath the surface, but a series of bubbles made a broken, blunted sound that indicated it had failed.

I trod water next to Holmes, who despite everything seemed rather sanguine.

"We are still trapped in here, you know," I said casually.

"I rather suspect the steel door was counterbalanced by one of the things I knocked over." He observed and we swam over and found we could lift it with ease, returning to the corridors.

We walked out of the front door of the Observatory soaking wet and exhausted to the sight of an amused looking Dr. Carlton-Rose and a confused looking Lestrade.

"So is Moriarty… alive?" Lestrade asked.

Holmes shook his head.

"I think not. He left a legacy of puzzles and madness but did not get to see it come to fruition."

"So the only puzzle he could not solve…" said Lestrade, "was death!"

Holmes reacted to this with more vehemence than when McKenzie revealed the bomb. We walked away, noting that Dr. Carlton-Rose had already left, and sought a carriage that would take our soggy bodies back home.

"I've had enough of puzzles," I said.

"Excellent, Watson. Then perhaps I shouldn't tell you… about the second deck."

THE END

SOLUTIONS

Puzzle 1: Forgery
6) The hot air balloon, was invented during Bewick's life. Everything else was invented after he died.

Puzzle 2: Railway Time
It is 1pm at London Charing Cross Station.

Puzzle 3: Dynamics of an Asteroid
1=C 2=A 3=B

Puzzle 4: Pianoforte
The answer is C.

Puzzle 5: Weights and Measures
Golden Sun=5, Silver Moon=2 and Iron Mars=1.

So, to balance perfectly, one side of the scales must have one Sun weight, two Moon weights and one Mars weight, and the other side must have one Sun weight, one Moon weight and three Mars weights.

Puzzle 6: The Path of Light
1C (mirrors reflect light rays back directly), 2B (concave lenses spread light rays), 3A (convex lenses converge light rays).

Puzzle 7: Anubis' Magic Square
The missing hieroglyphs are hand (3) and feather (4), making 7.

Puzzle 8: Kite String
It is string number 2.

Puzzle 9: Atmospheric Phenomena
1=B, 2=C, 3=A.

Puzzle 10: The Orrery
The answer is the ninth planet, Pluto which in 1891 had not been discovered or named yet and so was speculatively known as Planet X. Pluto was considered to be a planet from its discovery in 1930 until its demotion to 'dwarf planet' status in 2006.

Puzzle 11: Anamorphosis
It is Lord Nelson.

Puzzle 12: Shadow Gallery
The images are all flipped horizontally, as if in a mirror.

Puzzle 13: The Milliners
The answer is 2-the top hat, 3-the boater (suitable for town and country) and 5-the bowler hat. A mortar board is for academics and a deerstalker, despite its association with Holmes, is for wearing in the countryside.

Puzzle 14: Dancing Men?
The message reads "I CANNOT HELP, THE DETECTIVE IS NOT MY PROBLEM."

Puzzle 15: Constellations
The answer is 1C, 2B, 3A. The sum is the number of the stars in each: 7 x 3 + 9=30.

Puzzle 16: HMS *Knight*

A1-C2-E3-F5-G7-E8-C7-A8-B6-C8-E7-G8-E9-C10-B8-C6-E5-D3-
E1-G2-F4-E2-G1-F3-G5-F7-G9

Puzzle 17: A New Symbology

The answer is symbol 3.

Puzzle 18: No Puzzle?

The top half is a king of clubs but it says Q, not K. The bottom half
is a queen of diamonds and the number is K, not Q. The Queen also
has a moustache.

Puzzle 19: Serpents

Snake 3 is the matching snake.

Puzzle 20: Agriculture

The pictures are 1-a tomato, 2-corn on the cob, 3-a pumpkin, 4-some
rhubarb and 5-a cucumber.

The answer is the rhubarb, which is technically a vegetable, while
all the rest are technically fruits.

Puzzle 21: Train Journeys

The Stoke train arrives first. The Leeds train travels 190 miles at
80mph = 2 hours, 22 mins, 30 secs. Add 2 x 5 minute stops = 10
mins which makes 2 hours, 32 mins and 30 secs. The Stoke train
travels 155 miles at 80mph = 1 hour, 56 minutes, 15 seconds. Add 4
x 5 minute stops = 20 mins, which makes 2 hours, 16 minutes and
15 seconds.

Puzzle 22: A Hand

They represent a 'royal flush' in poker. 10, Jack, King, Queen, and
Ace (Sherlock)

Puzzle 23: A British Clipper Ship

There are 95 triangles in total.

Puzzle 24: Hounds

1-Great Dane, 2-*Canis Lupus* (Grey Wolf), 3-chow chow, 4-Dalmatian, 5-basset hound.

2 is the odd one out because it is not a dog.

Puzzle 25: Blackmailer's Safe

1=2 times, 2=3 times, 3=1 time and 4=4 times (because you must turn each dial at least once)

Puzzle 26: Rogue's Gallery

The answer is 1D, 2A, 3B, 4C.

Puzzle 27: The Queen's House

House 3's statement, "The Queen is not in residence in House 1", is true. The Queen is in residence in House 2.

Puzzle 28: Common Birds of the UK

1-Magpie, 2-Raven, 3-Crow, 4-Jackdaw and 5-Rook.

Puzzle 29: Omne Ignotum Pro Magnifico

A) His stubble indicates he was in a rush this morning. B) The train ticket tucked in his hat shows he anticipated falling asleep while on his journey. C) His distinctive Homburg hat (only popular in the UK from 1892 onwards) originates from Germany. D) His duelling scar indicates he has fenced frequently, which explains his typically brutal upper-class schooling. E) The mud on his trousers is from where he walked through the fields when his train broke down.

Puzzle 30: World

This card works in combination with puzzle 34. "The player passed seven men and scored" indicates the time 7:20 (a score is 20). The minute hand points at Australia, which is where the player is from.

Puzzle 31: Toxicology

The plants are 1-Yew, 2-Foxglove, 3-Potato, 4-Marigold, 5-Tobacco and 6-Oleander.

They match up with the poisons as such: A=2, B=3, C=6, D=5, E=1. Marigolds do not produce poison.

Puzzle 32: The Dancing Bear

Wind box 1 for 10 seconds. Plays for 30 seconds. Start winding box 2. After 30 seconds stop winding box 2, go back and wind box 1 for 10 seconds. That plays for 30 seconds as you finish winding box 2. As box 2 plays for 3 minutes you begin winding up box 3. After 3 minutes wind up box 1 for 10 seconds, then as that plays for 30 seconds wind up box 2 again, then stop after 30 seconds to wind box 1 again, then finish winding box 2, then as that plays for 3 minutes finish winding box 3, then box 3 plays for 12 minutes, which gives you the time to pick the lock.

Puzzle 33: A Peculiar Filing System

Each number is multiplied by itself, and then added to 2. The final number is 2,090,918.

Puzzle 34: Match

This card is solved in combination with card 30.

Puzzle 35: Apiculture

Worker bees are 10, Queen Bees are 5 and Larvae are 4, therefore, remembering the order of operations 10 + 5 x 4 = 30.

Puzzle 36: A Drop of Thames Water

Skull=7, Fish=32, Cat Head=45, so Skull x Fish - Cat Head =179

Puzzle 37: Dividing the Loot

Puzzle 38: Pie Chart

Moran = A, Bone Picker = C, Stiletto = D and Porlock= B.

Puzzle 39: High Stakes

5) Silver Blaze is the winner.

Silver Blaze: Does first 50 in 3 seconds, then runs rest in 1 minute 30, so 1 minute 33. (WINNER)

Basil's Boy: gets to halfway at 47 seconds, then takes a minute to run the second half so 1 minute 47 seconds (SECOND).

Jeremy's Hare: 1 minute 43 until last 100 yards then takes 6 seconds so 1 minute 49 (THIRD).

Benedictine: 1 minute 17 seconds then collapses after 1,500 yards so Does Not Finish (DNF).

Mickelwhite takes 1 minute 53. (FOURTH).

Puzzle 40: Philately

The queen on the second stamp in the middle row is wearing a string of pearls.

Puzzle 41: Denizens of Baker Street

220A – Sir Donald D'eath, the stabbing socialite

220B – Colonel Sebastian Moran, the hunter and assassin

221A– Mrs. Hudson

221B – Sherlock Holmes

222A –Emmanuel Strukov, taxidermist of humans

222B – Mrs. Hermione Bunn, the Droitwich poisoner

Puzzle 42: M

$1+1\times1+1+2-1\times1+3+3\div1+1\times4+6=20$

Puzzle 43: Floorplan for a Robbery

Use C to go into the kitchen, get the scissors/tin snips, then cut the alarm's wire, and then enter via D, which will allow you to bypass the corridor with the dog.

Puzzle 44: The Black Museum

1E, 2C, 3B, 4A and 5D.

Puzzle 45: Connections

They are all "pipes": 1-a Boatswain's pipe, 2-a diagram of the cross section of a "pipe", a type of metal casting defect, 3-a volcanic pipe (geological phenomenon), 4-a "pipe" sized cask, 5-a Hookah pipe

Puzzle 46: Nitroglycerin Plot

MB is the Bomb Maker, JMc is the transporter and SM is the guard. If JMc was the truth teller then that would mean MB is the liar, but then he wouldn't say he's not the guard. So either MB or SM are the truth teller, and SM would not say he is the liar, so it must be MB. SM would also not admit to being the liar if he was, so he must be the Guard, and JMc is the Transporter.

Puzzle 47: Dr. John Watson

The dried blood is actually ketchup because it is red and blood dries as a dark brown or black. The knife in his pocket is actually a doctor's lancet, recognizable from its shape. The money is in fact a prescription because it is clearly a handwritten note. The needle mark on the neck is a shaving cut as evident from the dried blood upon it. Moriarty's initials are JM, MM refers to Watson's former wife, Mary Morstan, from whom this is a keepsake.